The Proverbs of Alfred

Walter William Skeat, Alfred

LELAND·STANFORD·JVNIOR·VNIVERSITY

THE PROVERBS OF ALFRED

RE-EDITED FROM THE MANUSCRIPTS

BY THE

REV. WALTER W. SKEAT

Litt.D., LL.D., D.C.L., Ph.D., F.B.A.

ELRINGTON AND BOSWORTH PROFESSOR OF ANGLO-SAXON IN THE
UNIVERSITY OF CAMBRIDGE
AND FELLOW OF CHRIST'S COLLEGE

'Alfred the king,
Englelondes deorling.'
Layamon's Brut, i. 269.

OXFORD
AT THE CLARENDON PRESS
1907

HENRY FROWDE, M.A.
PUBLISHER TO THE UNIVERSITY OF OXFORD
LONDON, EDINBURGH
NEW YORK AND TORONTO

245111

PREFACE

My chief object in publishing a new edition of 'The Proverbs of Alfred' is to give, for the first time, a correct text of the more important and longer text contained in the Trinity College (Cambridge) MS., which has hitherto been very incorrectly reproduced, though it has already been issued three times.

At the same time, I give a full account of the peculiar errors of spelling due to the Anglo-French scribe, and tabulate and explain the strange forms which appear, not here only, but in many other texts of the thirteenth century as well. The importance of paying attention to such peculiarities may be illustrated by a single easy example. It is commonly said that the spelling *sal* for *shal* is a sure sign of a Northern dialect; but it is quite common in many Southern MSS., and occurs frequently, for example, in the later text of Layamon.

I also take occasion, at the same time, to print or collate such fragments of the Cotton MS. as have been preserved; and to add explanatory notes to the whole poem, together with remarks upon the grammar and the metre. The Glossarial Index is fuller than that in the English Text Society's edition, and, now that the right readings have been restored, explains many words for the first time.

CONTENTS

CONTENTS

INTRODUCTION

§ 1. The curious and early poem usually entitled 'The Proverbs of Alfred' exists in two different versions, the longer (and presumably the later) of which exceeds the shorter by 253 lines. In order to prevent ambiguity, I shall call the shorter version the A-text, and the longer one the B-text. (I add a fragment of a C-text at pp. 2–13, but it is not really an independent one; it is merely a variant of the B-text.) The B-text has never been previously presented to the reader with sufficient accuracy; and, in order to show how this has come about, it is necessary to describe the older printed editions.

§ 2. **Reliquiæ Antiquæ.** In 1841 appeared the well-known and interesting collection of certain Old and Middle English pieces with the following title:—'Reliquiæ Antiquæ, Scraps from Ancient MSS., illustrating chiefly Early English Literature and the English Language. Edited by Thomas Wright, Esq., M.A., F.S.A., and James Orchard Halliwell, Esq., F.R.S., F.S.A. 2 vols. London, 1841.' At pp. 170–88 of vol. i we find the following:—'THE PROVERBS OF KING ALFRED. From MS. Trin. Coll. Camb. B. 14. 39, of the beginning of the thirteenth century. There was also a copy in MS. Cotton, Galba A. xix, which unfortunately perished in the fire. Wanley (p. 231) and Spelman (Vit. Ælf. p. 127) have preserved some lines of it, which give some various readings. There is another copy in a MS. at Oxford, of which Sir Frederic Madden has kindly given a transcript, printed here at the foot of the pages.'

We find here, in fact, both texts. In the upper part of the

pages is Text B, from the Trinity MS.; and in the lower part is Text A, from the Jesus College MS. at Oxford. But *no* 'various readings' are given from the transcripts of the Cotton MS. Perhaps Mr. Wright had originally designed to give some (as seems to be implied), but the design was never carried out.

The Trinity MS. (of which more is said below) presents many difficulties, and the result is that Wright's text cannot be relied on.

The Jesus College MS. is clearly written, and the text (as printed by Wright) is fairly good. Nevertheless, it is incorrect in about nine instances, that need not be specified. The errors are not serious.

§ 3. Salomon and Saturnus. In 1848 appeared a work with the following title :—'The Dialogue of Salomon and Saturnus, with an Historical Introduction, by John M. Kemble, M.A. London; printed for the Ælfric Society, MDCCCXLVIII.' At pp. 225-57 we find a discussion of the Proverbs of Alfred, and at pp. 226-48 we again find Text B printed in full, from the Trinity MS. above-mentioned, accompanied by 'a rough translation of it, without which it would be scarcely intelligible'. There are no 'various readings', and Text A is not represented. Kemble's account of the poem is as follows.

'A curious poem, which once seems to have been a favourite in England, in which Ælfred, England's darling,[1] sustains the principal character, though not a dialogue, is on many accounts worthy of insertion here. It is a collection of wise sayings which that prince delivered to his Witena gemōt at Seaford. There was a MS. of this in the Cotton collection, Galba A. xix, which is now lost; a copy of it,

---

[1] Rather, 'darling of the Angles;' l. 11.

however, exists in the Bodleian;[1] a third[2] is found in the library of Lincoln[3] College, Oxford; and a fourth in Trin. Coll. Camb. B. 5. 19,[4] which is so curious a specimen of the language in the thirteenth century, that I take the following copy of it in preference to any other.[5] It is partly alliterative, partly in final rime, the couplets being thrown together in nearly the same careless manner as in Layamon.'

Kemble's text was evidently printed from a transcript which he made for himself. It would appear as if he consulted Wright's text when his proof-sheets were in type, as he repeats some of Wright's errors. It is only necessary to add here that his text cannot be relied upon, and that he has misunderstood several words and sentences; though his 'rough translation' is well worth consulting.

§ 4. **An Old English Miscellany.** In 1872 appeared An Old English Miscellany, edited by Dr. R. Morris, and printed for the Early English Text Society. It contains many poems from the Jesus College MS., one of which is The Proverbs of Alfred. Dr. Morris prints the two chief texts on opposite pages, at pp. 102–38. 'Text I' is that which I have called above the A-text, and is printed from the Jesus College MS. This text is unique, there being no other copy known. It therefore coincides, word for word, with the text previously printed by Wright in the Reliquiæ Antiquæ, as noted above; except that the printed text was carefully compared once more with the original MS., and the few

[1] It will be shown below that this copy, alas! gives but a few extracts; had it been at all complete, it would have been of much greater value.

[2] The word 'third' is odd; for as the two first mentioned give the very same text, it is really only a *second*.

[3] An obvious slip of memory; for 'Lincoln' read 'Jesus'.

[4] *Sic*; an error for B. 14. 19.

[5] But there was *no* other copy to be had, except that in the Jesus MS. Of the Cotton MS. only a few scraps are preserved.

errors eliminated. I have again compared it with the MS., but found nothing to alter; the absurd reading *werende* for *wexende* in l. 438 is so miswritten in the MS. itself. See the description of this MS. below, in § 5.

Dr. Morris's 'Text II' is that which I have called above the B-text. No notice is taken of the Cotton MS. (doubtless, on account of the fragmentary nature of the late transcripts of it), and the editor's design was to give the text of the Trinity MS. only. Unfortunately, this MS. was, in 1872, quite inaccessible; it had disappeared from the College library, and was supposed to be lost. The story of its recovery is given below, under the description of the MS. See § 6.

Under the circumstances, Dr. Morris did the best thing possible. He carefully collated the prints by Wright and Kemble, and thus compiled a text of his own, giving the readings of Wright and Kemble in the margin. But the spellings of the MS. (as explained below) are so extraordinary that he could not but miss the meaning in several cases; and the chief object of the present reprint is to set the difficulties right. How great were these difficulties is best shown by the note 5 at the bottom of p. ix of the editor's preface, where he says:—' It is somewhat strange that Kemble and Wright should have both, in very many cases, mistaken a short stumpy *g* for an *s*. In one instance [in l. 134] where Kemble reads *gise*, Wright has *guge* for *gunge*, and that this is the correct reading is proved by Text I, which has *yong*.' But the true solution is quite different. There is no 'short stumpy *g*' here, but only the character represented in print by ȝ. The word is actually written 'ȝise', which Kemble intentionally printed as 'gise'; the word is slightly smudged, but Wright should not have read it as 'guge'. The fact that he did so suggested the form 'gu[n]ge' in Morris's text. It is needless to say more upon this point, as the MS. is fully described below, in § 7.

The 'Old English Miscellany' contains no Notes, but there is a good Glossarial Index to the numerous pieces which are there printed.

§ 5. The MS. in Jesus College, Oxford. Having enumerated all former editions, it is now time to describe the MSS.

MS. no. 29 in the library of Jesus College, Oxford, now transferred to the Bodleian Library, is one of great interest. It contains copies of a considerable number of Old English texts of the thirteenth century, all of which are printed in An Old English Miscellany (see § 4), with the exception of the long poem entitled The Owl and the Nightingale. The contents of the MS. may be thus briefly described.

It consists really of *two* MSS. of quite different dates; the former is no older than the fifteenth century, and contains a Chronicle ending as late as 1445. The latter is of the thirteenth century, the chief contents being as follows.

1. Poem no. I in O. E. Misc. [Old English Miscellany].
2. The Owl and the Nightingale.
3. Poems in O. E. Misc., in the following order :—II–V; XX, XXI; VI, VII; XXII–XXV; VIII–XVIII.
4. Assisa panis Anglie (Latin ; short).
5. Ici comence de Tobye (Anglo-French).
6. Poem no. XIX in O. E. Miscellany.
7. Pieces in Anglo-French.

Of these, The Proverbs of Alfred is poem no. XV; beginning at leaf 262 (formerly 189). Text A (occurring in this MS. only) extends to 456 lines, as numbered by Morris; and I have adhered to his numbering as closely as was possible, for convenience of reference.[1]

[1] It was found unadvisable to adhere to it throughout, but the

Text A is considerably shorter than Text B, and there seems to be no reason why we may not regard it as representing (in a somewhat late copy) the earlier text of the two. Further remarks on this subject will be found below. Cf. note to l. 17, on p. 54.

The spelling is reasonably good and sufficiently regular; but there are just a few traces that betray the Norman scribe. Once he inserts *h* in the wrong place, as in *hiselþe* for *iselþe*, 362. He writes *w* for *u* in *hw* (how), 31, 71; and *w* for *wu* in *wrþsiþes*, 32, *wrþie*, 60, 404, *iwrche*, 130, *wrt*, 168, *wrþe*, 184; but the latter mistake is less frequent towards the end of the poem. He writes *re* for *r* in *clerek*, 19, 78, *chyreche*, 373. Other errors appear in *swyhc* for *swych*, 239; *ischolte* for *ischote*, 421; *londle* for *londe*, 379; *loþ* for *leþ*, 333; *werende* for *wexende*, 438.

Further, *vouh* is for *veoh*, 192; *one* is for *on* (prep.), 106; *frumþe* in l. 129 is a downright blunder for *fremde*; and *Mayþenes* for *madmes* (as in l. 198) is hardly excusable. There is enough to show that the scribe was simply copying from an older MS. which he now and then misread. In one place he has committed an error in judgement, viz. in l. 340; where he first of all wrote *nys*, and afterwards erased the initial *n*, which happens to be necessary for the sense. But these are small matters and this Text stands in startling contrast to Text B, in which so many curious errors abound.

§ 6. The Trinity MS. This is MS. B. 14. 39 in the library of Trinity College, Cambridge. As stated above, it was missing in 1872, when Dr. Morris printed his edition.

---

numbering of the lines in the present volume seldom differs from that in Morris's text by more than 1 or 2. Line 152 is accidentally omitted in Text A. A line is lost again after l. 214. Lines 233 and 234 were counted by Morris as *one*; so also were ll. 400, 400*. Something is wrong with l. 364 and the next one. The colophon at the end of text A was counted as l. 457!

It was at one time supposed to have been stolen, but it had only gone astray, as was explained by Mr. W. Aldis Wright in a letter which appeared in *The Times* of July 13, 1896. In company with some printed books belonging to the same library, it was accidentally packed up and sent away to a former fellow of the college. It so happened that the parcel was never opened, and after thirty-three years was returned to the college without having been interfered with. Mr. Aldis Wright had suspected that some of the college books had thus gone astray, and wrote to inquire about them; whereupon he not only regained the books which he sought, but, much to his astonishment, found the long-lost MS. amongst them.

At a meeting of the Philological Society on May 7, 1897, I read a paper upon the peculiarities of this MS., which is printed in the Transactions of that Society for 1895-8, p. 399. Many of the remarks which here follow are repeated from the account there given, but with a few corrections. By way of showing the nature of the difficulties with which Morris had to contend, I drew attention to l. 295 [294 of Text II in Morris] where the scribe had to write the word *trewe*, corresponding to *treowe* in Text A. The word he actually wrote was *ter*, which makes no sense. Probably Wright so copied it, but made a note that *tre* may have been meant; at any rate, his printer made it appear as *tertre*. Next, Kemble probably copied it correctly also, but afterwards consulted Wright's text; at any rate, the result which he gives us is *ter tre*, as two words, which he explains by ' a tree '. Morris naturally supposed that the MS. really had some such form, and printed *tertre* in the text, and *ter tre* in the margin; in fact, there was nothing else to be done. And his Glossary necessarily has the record:—' Tertre, (?) read *tre*=tree.' See my note upon the passage.

§ 7. Peculiarities of the Trinity MS. An examination of the MS. soon showed that the scribe must have been a Norman, who no doubt did his best to reproduce an old copy which he had before him ; but his knowledge of English was so slight that he did not even know the value of some of the English characters ! This singular fact admits of positive proof; for, as Mr. Aldis Wright pointed out to me, we find at the foot of the first page of the poem, the following remarkable note :—

iẏe   w   ant   iþorn

ʒ   ƿ   ꝛ   þ

The meaning of this is obvious and significant. Before the scribe began to write out the poem, he made a note of four new characters which he had to employ. These were: ʒ, ƿ, ꝛ, þ. And he noted their meaning in the following manner. The name of the first was *ye* (pronounced as mod. E. *yea*) ; but he was unable to sound the initial *y* without prefixing the slight vowel-sound *i*. The second symbol was the A. S. symbol for *w*; so he wrote over it the early Norman *w*, made of two interlaced *v*'s. The third was the A. S. symbol for *and*, which he characteristically pronounced as *ant*. And the fourth was the A.S. symbol for *th*, usually called *thorn* ; but here again he found it convenient to prefix an *i*, as before. Having learnt (as he supposed) his lesson, he promptly began his work. But he had by no means learnt his lesson aright. He uses ꝛ freely and correctly, for he had only to reproduce it ; but he was quite unable to distinguish the A. S. *w* from the A. S. *th*, and frequently misuses them. But the strangest part of the story is that he could not remember the meaning of ʒ, and constantly uses it in the place of *w* ! This is the real clue to many very extraordinary readings. Thus, in l. 182, all the printed copies have *gerlde*; but the MS. has *ʒerlde*, a playful variant of *werlde*, which is obviously meant; the

A-text has *world.* So also, in l. 145, the printed texts have *rogen*, but the MS. has *roȝen*, for *rowen.* And in l. 147, Kemble prints *sginkin*, because the MS. has *sȝinkin*, meaning *swinkin.* Here the correction is so obvious that Wright prints it as *swinkin*; but he makes no remark as to the spelling of the MS. It is a fault of all the printed editions that they print every ȝ as *g*, making no distinction between the sounds of these symbols; so that even when the scribe correctly writes *ȝu*, meaning ' you', and *ȝure*, meaning ' your', in ll. 28, 29, the editions give us the unphonetic forms *gu* and *gure*!

§ **8. How to correct the scribal errors.** We have seen that the scribe confuses ȝ with *w*, and *w* with þ (*th*); and there is a large number of instances of this kind, in which the right reading is certain and obvious, especially where we have the help of Text A. As it is absurd to admit into the text such elementary mistakes, I usually give the right form in the text, and the mistaken one in the footnote. As the distinction, in the MS., between the Norman *w* and the A.S. þ is frequently made and ought to be recognised, I print the former as an ordinary ' w', and the latter as ' *w* ' in italics; for the use of þ is undesirable in a Middle-English text, since there is always a tendency to confuse it with þ. In such a case as that wherein the MS. has ' sȝinkin', I print the corrected form as ' swinkin', in order to show at once the nature of the scribe's error; of course the word was 'swinkin ' or ' swinken ' in the copy which he had before him.

But the fact that the scribe was doubtful as to the correct use both of sounds and symbols, renders it necessary to do much more than this. Now that we know that we have a Norman to deal with, it is both necessary and easy to make a full tabulation of all his peculiarities of speech. And it is sufficient to give here the results of the investigation. They are the more useful because mistakes of a similar kind are extremely common in MSS. of the thirteenth century, as, e. g. in the unique MS. of the Lay of Havelok. In fact, I have already given similar tables in my Preface to the Oxford edition of Havelok printed in 1902; and therefore number the sources of error precisely as they are numbered there, for convenience of reference. See that Preface, pp. x–xviii.

§ 9. Table of sounds misrepresented : initial sounds.

1. The Norman misuses initial *h*. Hence we find *herles* for *erles*, 5. So also *heke*, 9, 33; *helfred*, 73, 118; *herl*, *heþeling*, 74; *huuele*, 135; and many more. On the other hand, we find *is* for *his*, 58, 204, 206, 207; *biouit* for *bihouith*, 87; &c.

2. Old French had no initial *sh*. The Norman often wrote *s* instead. Exx. *sulin* for *shulin*, 16; *sal* for *shal*, 57, 83, 166, 173, 262. So also *salt*, 394; *saltu*, 358; *sule*, 71; *sullen*, 188, 202; *sollen*, 201; *sold*, 277; *solde*, 279. So also *wrsipe* for *wurshipe*, 32; *fles* for *flesh*, 470. In other cases, the scribe wrote *sc* for *sh*; as in *scapen*, 143; *scal*, 163; *scullen*, 179, 191; *scolde*, 289; *iscoten*, 421. So also in *Idilscipe*, 286. And note *frendchipe*, 373, 620. Hence *sal* and *scal* both represent *shal*.

3. Old French had no initial *th*. Hence the Anglo-French scribes adopted the A.S. þ as a new symbol. But our scribe could not always remember its value, and sometimes actually uses it in place of ȝ. Hence we find *þif* for *ȝif*, 65, 398, &c.; *leþen* for *leȝen*, to lie, 368; *liþen* for *liȝen*, 670.[1] Conversely, we even find ȝ written for þ; as *wraȝed* for *wraþed*, 276. See 6 (below).

---

[1] It is hopeless to explain such words unless these misspellings are understood. Morris explains *liþen* by 'listen', which would be quite correct if *liþen* were really meant. But it is not, as Kemble perceived; for he explains it by 'be slippery'!

Neither is this the end of the trouble; for the written characters for þ and the A.S. ƿ (*w*) are so much alike that there are certainly cases in which one has been miswritten for the other. Thus, in l. 182, the MS. has 'i *wis* ȝerlde'; but the A-text has 'in þis world', which is obviously right. Again, in l. 623, the MS. perhaps has 'bet him siȝwen' for 'bet him siþen'; but I have not noted it, as it may be also read as standing for the latter form; the characters cannot always be distinguished. The former editions all have 'bet him siwen', but the editors cannot explain it; Kemble says: 'and better be silent thereby, that it begin to plague him,' which is nonsense. The right sense is easy enough, when the correction is made; it is: 'and beat him afterwards therewith (at the time), that he may begin to smart'; see the note. There is no such word as *siwen*; 'to be silent' is expressed by *swien* or *swiȝen* (A. S. *swīgian*).

As to þ when it occurs finally, see 15 (below).

4. The E. initial *hw* or *wh* became, for the Norman, a mere *w*. Hence we find *wad* for *hwat*, 131; *wenne* for *hwenne* (A. *hwanne*), 178; *wile* for *hwile*, 311*, 393, 431; *wen* for *hwen*, 655. So also *wo* for *hwo*, 59; *wu* for *hwu* or *hu* (how), 71. The confusion is complete when the scribe writes, conversely, *hwendes* for *wendes*, 569.

5. The Norman scribes write *w* for *wu*, initially. Hence we find *wrsipe*, 32; *wrþin*, 60; *unwrd* for *unwurþ*, 120; *wrþe*, 571; *wld*, 681. Much more extraordinary is the use of *w* for *uu = vu*, as in *wrþere* for *vurþere* (A. *furþer*), 128; and actually *wuidewis* for *widewis*, 593. In l. 400*, the word *wis* (wise) is written *uuis* (with *uu = w*); whilst in l. 531 we find *euuere* for *euere* (with *uu = v*). Lastly, initial *wi* is written *vi*, as in *ville*, 295; *vimmon*, 340; *visle*, 489.

6. Initial *y* (consonant) is sometimes dropped, but not here. We find the forms ȝu, you, ȝure, your, correctly written. Yet

in l. 278 *h* is substituted for ӡ, in the form *liuihinde.* The use of the A.S. form of *w* for ӡ, or conversely, is a graphic error, due to a forgetfulness of the true force of the symbol. Surprising though it be, there are several instances of it, as in *we* for *ӡe,* 14, 27 ; *sawin* for *saӡin,* 631. And conversely, *saӡin* for *sawin,* 123 ; *roӡen* for *rowen,* 145 ; *sӡinkin* for *swinkin,* 147 ; *ӡerlde* for *werlde,* 182 ; *ӡise* for *wise,* 134, 136. So in l. 31, *ӡu* is put for *wu* or *hwu* (how), also spelt *hu.* See 3 (above).

§ 10. **Medial sounds.** The chief one to be noticed is *r.*

7. It is remarkable that some A.F. scribes express the trill of the *r* by inserting a vowel after it. Examples are: *cleric* for *clerc,* 19 ; *cherril* for *cherl,* 92 ; *arren* for *arn,* 582. In ll. 589, 625, I allow the forms *barin, baren* (for *barn*) to stand, as the strong trilling of the *r* is essential to the metre.

Similarly, we find a vowel inserted after *l* in *weleþe* for *welþe,* 220 (cf. l. 217) ; and *salit* for *salt,* 470. In l. 462, *ale* should be *alle.*

§ 11. **Final sounds.** The Norman scribes had difficulties with such final sounds as *gh, ght, ld, lk, nd, ng, nk, t,* and *th.* Several of these are ill expressed in the Trinity MS.

8. The final guttural (A. S. *h*) is sometimes denoted by *ch.* Exx. *þuruch,* for *þuruh,* 206 ; *þurch,* 361 ; *inoch,* 523. So also *achte,* for *ahte,* 250, 254 ; *hachte,* for *ahte,* 522 ; *þochte,* for *þohte,* 293. A worse symbol is *c,* as in *þauc,* for *þauh,* 283.

9. The final *ht* (A.S. *ht*) caused still greater difficulty. The symbols for it are no less than *seven,* viz. *st, t, th, ct, tht, dt,* and *ch* ! Exx. (1) *mist,* 155, 239, 392, 619 ; *mistin,* 31 ; *misten,* 597 ; *dristin,* 42, 203 ; *ristewis,* 55 ; *risten,* 596.[1] (2) *cnit* (for *cniht*), 78 ; *nout,* 128, 201, 669, 706 ; *nowit,* 284 ; *brit,* 306 * ; *douter,* 550. (3) *cnith,* 87 ; *noth,* 318. (4) *rict,* 79 ;

---

[1] In the combination *st,* the *s* is usually the long *s* (ſ).

Acte, 185. (5) *litht,* 566 ; *mitht,* 648. (6) *widt,* for *wiht,* 443. (7) *drichen,* for *drihten,* 517. The last is doubtless miswritten for *drichten,* but this does not lessen the variety, as *cht* for *ht* occurs nowhere else in this text.

10. Final *l* for *ld* occurs in Havelok. So also here is *chil* for *child,* 430. Cf. *weleþe, salit,* in 7 (above).

11. Final *l* and *lek,* both for *lk,* occur in Havelok. Some difficulty as to final *lk* seems to be hinted at by the spelling *folck* (for *folk*), 590.

12. In Havelok, final *nd* appears as *nt* or *n* ; so that *and* appears as *ant* or *an.* The scribe of the present text gives us *ant* for *and* in his footnote (§ 7). But he goes further, and writes *t* for *d* ; as in *alfret,* 195 ; *mit,* 275, 620 ; *isait,* 329 ; *middellert,* 389 ; *aquet* (for *a qued*), 702. *Wenne,* for *wende,* 434, is a surprising example. And note *lestind,* altered to *lestin,* 474.

13. Final *ng* and *nk* were likewise difficult sounds. *Ng* appears as *nh* in *kinhis,* 2, *þinhes,* 48, *brinhit,* 259 ; *brinhin,* 668. Also as *nc* ; in *kinc,* 36. And lastly, as *nk* ; in *enkelonde,* 12, 17 ; *þinke,* 278, 354, 600 ; *tunke,* 282, 425 ; *sinken,* 355 ; *wronke,* 596 ; *lonke,* 692. Conversely, *nk* appears as *ng* ; as in *biþeng,* 400 ; *þeng,* 518.

14. It is common in Havelok to find *th* written for *t* ; but I only observe one example of this in the present text, viz. in l. 626, where *sittest* is written *sitthest.* Of course, the *th* here only means a kind of aspirated *t,* not the A.S. þ in *þorn.*

15. Final *th* is represented, in a large number of instances, either by *d,* as in *hauid,* 205, *god,* 217, *sed,* 236, &c. ; or else by *t,* as in *þenket,* 60, *souit,* 82, *biouit* (for *bihouiþ*), 87. Perhaps we may conclude that, in the former set, the original had *hauið, goð, seð,* &c. ; and in the latter set *þenkeþ, soweþ,* &c.

Two most extraordinary cases occur ; in one of these the final *th* appears as *dþ,* viz. in *falewidþ,* 579 ; and in the other case as *cd*, viz. in *cherricd*, 85. Such spellings well illustrate the difficulty of sounding the E. *þ*.

§ 12. **Other variations.** But the above variations do not exhaust the peculiarities of this unique MS. I here collect a few more variants, such as are not very commonly seen elsewhere.

(*a*) A dotted *y* sometimes appears in place of *w*. Thus *syiþe, troyþe*, 196, 506 (the *y* dotted in both instances) really mean *swiþe* and *trowþe*. In the first instance, all the editions have *swiþe*; in the second, Wright has *troyþe*, and Kemble *trogþe*.

(*β*) *Ch* occurs for *c*, and *c* for *ch*; as in *Ach*, for *Ac* (but), 149; and *Hic* for *Ich* (I), 706.

(*γ*) *G* (with the sound of *j*) occurs for *ch*; as in *adige*, for *a diche* (a ditch), 700; *sug* (i. e. *suj*), for *such*, 676.

(*δ*) Final *d* constantly appears for *t*. Thus *þad=þat*, 24, 41, 139, &c.; *wid = wit*, 221; *wad = wat = hwat*, 131; *id = it*, 132; *hid = hit* (it), 329, 650; *bold = bolt*, 421; *ard = art*, 589.

(*ε*) *U* between two vowels usually stands for *v*. But here it may stand for *w*; as in *laueliche*, for *laweliche*, 77; *souit*, for *sowiþ*, 82; *mouin*, 83; *cnouen*, 88; *souin*, 93. In l. 294, the scribe at first wrote *beuen*, but afterwards corrected it to *bewen* (with A.S. *w*), as though it had just dawned upon him that *w* was better.

(*ζ*) Conversely, he uses the A.S. *w* (never the French one) with the force of *v*! See *hawe*, for *haue = have*, 418; so also *hawest*, 198; *hewit*, 366; *hawen*, 304, 614; *newere*, 221; *newir*, 222; *hewere* (ever), 689; *iwil* (evil), 703; *Lewe*, 661; *lowien*, 599; *ower*, 600; *selwe*, 426, &c.

I have now mentioned most of the more important peculiarities; there is no difficulty about such a form as *swist* (second *s* a long *s*), since it is often miswritten for *swift*.

§ 13. Some Vowel-sounds. It is, however, important to remark that even the vowel-sounds are often badly rendered. The common blunder of confusing *e* and *o* is not absent. Thus *no*, 169, means *ne* (nor); and *boþ*, 407, means *beþ*.[1]

Conversely, *knewen*, 358, means the infinitive *knowen*; and *þe*, 548, means *þo*, i. e. those. Kemble translates this *þe* by 'them', and Morris by 'those'; but surely the form should be *þo*.

The A.S. *ǣht*, property, possessions, appears as *achte*, 250, 254, written for *ahte*. The form *haite*, 665, means *aihte*, which is an occasional form of *ahte* (see Stratmann); but *ahte* is preferable.

In 33, the form *salle* stands for *saulle*, or rather *saule*, souls.

In 460, *eþer* should rather be *eyþer* or *eiþer*.

In 635, *sete* is an error for *site*, 'sit thou.'

In 670, *liþen* is miswritten for *liȝen*; in 368, *leþen* is miswritten for *leȝen*. However both forms occur elsewhere, viz. *liȝen* and *leȝen*, in the sense 'to tell lies'.

In 635, *seiþen* should rather be *siþen*; and conversely, *siȝe* (I say), in 706, should rather be *seiȝe*.

In 542, *þin* is written *þiin* (thine); the *i* is long, but the double *i* is unusual.

The use of the suffix *-is* for *-es*, as in *biscop-is*, 3, occurs repeatedly. So also the use of *-in* for *-en*, as in *ler-in*, 13. These characteristic forms are, of course, retained.

§ 4. Noticeable errors of an exceptional kind. A few strange errors are worthy of notice, to render the sketch of the contents of the MS. more complete.

83. The MS. has *alsuipich*. Here *p* is miswritten for the

---

[1] I. e. shall be. The scribe has absurdly inserted *is*, so that the verb occurs twice over! Kemble seems to have noticed this, for he translates 'is boþ' by 'is'. Morris was unable to solve the puzzle, since his glossary explains *both* by '(?) booth, tabernacle'.

A.S. *w* (which it resembles), and the form meant is *alsuiwich*, in which *ui* is mistakenly repeated as *wi*. The word meant is *alsuich* or *alswich*, which is merely the two words *al suich* (all such, just such) run together.

123. The MS. has *and he as heȝed saȝin*, for *and he is heuede* (or *hauede*) *sawin*; compare the reading of the James MS., and see the Note.

126. The MS. has *on þe rerþe* (2nd *r* above the line); for *on þer erþe*, 'on the earth.'

169. The MS. has *wdode*, for *wode*; the *d* is accidentally repeated before the *o*.

295. The MS. has *ter*, as explained above (p. xiii).

318. The MS. has *Aretu*; see footnote and Note on p. 62.

321. MS. *iwrarþed* (first *r* above the line). It means that the second *r* should have *preceded* the *a*; so that *iwraþed* is intended.

341. MS. *cnoswen* (with long *s*); an *s* has been accidentally inserted.

359. MS. reading as in the footnote.

407. See footnote; and the note at pp. 64–5.

469. See footnote; the MS. is obviously faulty.

561. See footnote.

615. MS. *mestes*; obviously for *metes*.

634. MS. *wid*; but *d* is written for *t* so often that *wit* may well be intended. The correct form is *wite* (dissyllabic), representing the A.S. *wita*.

654. MS. indistinct; either *dett* or *deit*; the form meant is *dēþ*, i. e. 'doth.'

676. MS. *mod*, with a curl to the right of *d*; meaning uncertain.

§ 15. The James copy of the Cotton MS. Kemble says, as already noted, that 'there was a MS. of this [The

Proverbs of Alfred] in the Cotton collection, Galba A. xix, which is now lost; a copy of it, however, exists in the Bodleian'. Upon this Gropp remarks: 'In this he must be mistaken, no mention of any such copy occurring elsewhere.' Such has long been the general opinion; but I am greatly indebted to Prof. Dr. W. Heuser, of Göttingen, for referring me to MS. James 6, in the Bodleian Library. Indeed, Prof. Heuser did me the still greater favour of generously lending me his own transcript of the MS. I have myself no doubt (in spite of all such discrepancies as are noticed below) that this MS. is the one to which Kemble refers, and that it was copied from the Cotton MS. This is probably the reason why it is written throughout in A.S. characters; for we learn from Wanley that the Cotton MS. was likewise so written; see § 17 below. I am kindly informed by Mr. F. Madan, of the Bodleian Library, that this MS. James 6 contains various copies made by Mr. Richard James early in the seventeenth century. There is a note at the end of the piece that it was taken from a MS. belonging to Mr. Th. Allen. Mr. Allen died in 1633, and left all his MSS. to Sir Kenelm Digby; and some of these were bequeathed by the latter to the Bodleian. The particular Allen MS. in question is doubtless that now known as MS. Digby 4, which once contained ' Alfredi Regis Parabolæ ', though this piece has now disappeared from the volume; see the Catalogue of Digby MSS., col. 5.[1] That is to say, Allen's transcript is lost, and what we now have, viz. MS. James 6, is not a copy made at firsthand, but a copy of a copy, which allows more room for variation. And unfortunately it turns out that MS. James 6 does not give the whole poem, but only *extracts* taken here and there, viz. 68

---

[1] MS. James 6 (says Mr. Madan) was catalogued in print in Bernard's Old Catalogue of 1697, vol. i. part i. p. 258. The piece is there indicated by ' Ex Alfredi Concionibus, Saxonice; p. 68 '.

lines out of the first 98, and 51 lines elsewhere; about 119 lines in all, out of 709. More exactly, it contains lines 1–34, 41–2, 63–72, 74–83, 87–98, 119–32, 248–51, 258–9, 306–11, 298–301, 516–32, 335–6, 425–6, 652–3 (in this order).

§ 16. **The Spelman copy of the Cotton MS.** We have two other copies of extracts from the same Cotton MS. At p. 93 of Ælfredi Magni Vita, by Sir John Spelman (Oxford, 1678),[1] the author says that he was favoured with a transcript of the Cotton MS. made by Sir Thomas Cotton himself.[2] He then proceeds to give extracts, evidently with great inaccuracy, at pp. 94, 95. Here again, we have but a copy of a copy, printed by one who unfortunately despised the spelling of the MS.; 'ipsum exemplar adeo mendosum est, et tam scriptura Hybrida, quam sermone semibarbaro, ut nisi impudenter veritati vim facerem, non ausim publico committere, ad istius exemplaris fidem, quod penes me descriptum habeo.' He then says that the copy contains 31 sections; but as he does not count section 1 (as it is introductory), he really means 32. It therefore agrees with the B-text (as is otherwise evident); and contained all but a small portion at the end. The passage thus preserved is here printed as the C-text, containing ll. 1–98. Spelman next gives a Latin rendering of these lines; and afterwards, being by this time ashamed of the 'semibarbarous language' of the poem, gives a *Latin version only* of the sections corresponding to B. 6, B. 7, B. 14, B. 28, B. 29, B. 30. The last of these he calls section 29, so that it perhaps ended with l. 659.

§ 17. **The Wanley copy.** Lastly, in Wanley's Catalogue of Anglo-Saxon MSS., in the second volume of Hickes'

---

[1] A posthumous work. Sir John died in 1643.
[2] The collector of the Cotton MSS. was Sir Robert Bruce Cotton, who died in 1631, when they passed into the hands of his son, Sir Thomas Cotton. Sir Thomas Cotton's transcript may be dated as having been made between 1631 and 1643, when Spelman died.

Thesaurus (Oxford, 1705), we find a good transcript of the
first 30 lines of the Cotton MS., of which by that time (we
do not know why) only a small fragment was left [1]. Wanley's
words, at p. 231, are as follows :—' Galba A. xix. Frag-
mentum membr. pusillum Poeticè litteris Normanno-Saxonicis
circa temp. Henrici II. aut Ricardi I. conscriptum, in quo
continentur quædam ex Proverbiis et Apophthegmatis Ælfredi
Regis sapientissimi. Fol. 1. *Incip.* At Sifforde ', &c.

§ 18. **Collation of · the three copies.** On comparing
MS. James 6 with Wanley, we find, in the course of these
30 lines, very few variations, even in the spelling. The
following is the complete list, in which I denote the former
by J. and the latter by W. 6. J. *inserts* ꝼ *before* cnihtes.
7. J. erle ; W. erl. 9. J. *inserts* ꝼ *before* ec. 11. J. engla ; W.
Engle. 12. J. Englond ; W. Engelonde. 13. J. leren ; W.
laren. 20. J. luvede ; W. luuede. 21. J. worde ; W. word.
22. J. ware ; W. war. 23. J. wiseste ; W. wisest. 24. J. on
Engelond ; W. on Engelond on. 25. J. þus ; W. Ðus.

These are small matters ; whilst on the other hand, both
J. and W. agree as to such spellings as *swuðe* (for *swiðe*), 8 ;
Alfrede (with an otiose final *e*), 9 ; *swiðe*, 18.

I have no hesitation in concluding that the James MS. was
a copy (at secondhand, be it remembered) of scrappy extracts
made from no other than the Cotton MS. at a time when
that MS. was still unmutilated. And it is curious to note
that Spelman, who expressly says that he follows that MS.,
provides us with *a much longer set of variations,* as follows
(denoting Spelman's print by S.). 1. S. Sifford ; W. Sifforde.
2. S. Thaines ; W. þeines. S. many ; W. manie. 4. S. *inserts*
ꝼ *before the second* fele. 5. S. Earles ; W. Erles. 6. S.

---

[1] It was complete (or nearly so) in Spelman's time, and therefore in
Allen's time, which was earlier. It must have suffered mutilation
between 1643 and 1705.

Knihts; W. Cnihtes. S. egloche; W. egleche. 7. S. Erle; W. Erl. 8. S. swuth; W. swuðe. 9. S. *inserts* ꝺ *before* ec. S. Alfred; W. Alfrede. 12. S. Englond; W. Engelonde. 13. S. leren; W. laren. 14. S. him; W. hi. 19. S. Clerk; W. Clerc. 20. S. loved Gods werk; W. luuede Godes werc. 22. S. spech; W. speche. 23. S. wiseste; W. wisest. 24. S. on Englond; W. on Engelond on. 25. S. Thus quath; W. Ðus cwað. S. Alvered; W. Alured. 27. S. the; W. ꝫe. S. liben; W. liþen. 28. S. loverd; W. Louerd. 29. S. you; W. ꝫu. 30. S. wiseliche winges; W. wisliche þinges. Here are 29 variations instead of 12; and it is worth notice, further, that in 5 instances, both S. and J. agree as against Wanley, viz. in lines 9, 12, 13, 23, 24. It is difficult to believe in Wanley's spelling *laren*, in l. 13, which looks like an error of the press.

§ 19. **Method of printing the Texts.** The description of the MSS. has necessarily been a long one, because the facts relating to them are complicated and unusual. But it is easy to explain the texts as here printed.

A-text. The A-text, printed from the Jesus College MS., occupies the left-hand page (or part of the page) as far as it goes; ending at the bottom of p. 40. It only extends to 456 lines, according to the old numbering. As it is, in general, sufficiently good, only a very few corrections have been made, which are duly accounted for in the footnotes.

B-text. The B-text, printed from the Trinity College MS., occupies the right-hand page (or part of the page) throughout the first 450 lines; ending at the bottom of p. 41. After that, it is allowed to occupy *both* pages, to save space. It must be particularly observed that, in order to show its parallelism with the A-text, it was necessary to dislocate the order in which the sections appear in the MS. But that order is clearly shown by the *numbering* of the sections, in thick type, at the beginning of each. As this text abounds with errors of spelling of many kinds, it was considered advisable to restore it, throughout, so as to show the forms which the scribe, in all probability, had before him. All such corrections are accounted for in the footnotes. This text, be it observed, does not contain ll. 99–117, nor ll. 451–6. After l. 118, various readings are given in the footnotes from J. (MS. James 6), where possible; but the extant portions of the text in that MS. are few and scrappy, and often far apart (p. xxiv).

C-text. The C-text, printed from extant transcripts of the lost Cotton MS., only extends, continuously, for 98 lines, and occupies the lower part of pages 1–13. After that, mere fragments exist, in the 'James' transcript only, and supply the variants marked 'J.', as given in the footnotes to B.

It is only called 'C-text' for he sake of clearness. It is really *the same as* the B-text, with which it agrees very closely. It evidently had the sections *in precisely the same order*, as appears from the James MS. and from Spelman's remarks.

§ 20. Order of the Sections. The order of the sections in the earlier and later (or, at any rate, the shorter and longer) texts, is shown in the following tables :

A.	B. C.		B. C.	A.
1–5	1–5		1–5	1–5
6	.		.	6
7–9	6–8		6–8	7–9
10	10		9	11
11	9		10	10
12–14	11–13		11–13	12–14
15, 16	16, 17		14	23
17	21 *and* 20		15	.
18	25		16, 17	15, 16

A.	B. C.	B. C.	A.
19	19	18	.
20	23	19	19
21	29	21 *and* 20	17
22	26	22	.
23	14	23	20
.	15, 18, 22	24	.
.	24, 27, 28	25	18
.	30–37	26	22
		27, 28	.
		29	21
		30–37	.

§ 21. **Grammatical notes: Nouns.** The following examples of grammatical details are all taken from the A-text, as being more trustworthy. The following are examples of sbs. which are etymologically dissyllabic, and in which the final *-e* forms a distinct syllable. Nominatives: *hurde*, 10; *lawe*, 97; *elde*, 112, spelt *ealde*, 441; *vnhelþe*, 113; *weole*, 120; *wyse*, 136; *heorte*, 246; *tunge*, 425. To these add *blisse*, 396, 428; in which the A.S. nom. *bliss*, being feminine, was superseded by the form *blisse*, representing all the oblique cases.

The following are datives: *Seuorde*, 1; *lawe*, 8; *londe*, 12; *werke*, 22; *louerde*, 28; *dure*, 85; *knyhte*, 87, governed by *bihoueþ* (cf. the phr. *to behove to one* in N.E.D.); *youhþe*, 100, 149; *i-vere*, 219, 223; *ore*, 241; *a-lyue*, 260; *bure*, 309; *horse*, 313; *balewe*, 397.

The following are accusatives: *vrre*, 205; *tunge*, 282; *sawe*, 361; *iselþe*, 362; *lesinge*, 363; *worlde* (A.S. *weorulde*, f. acc.), 389; *wunne* (see Stratmann), 390; *wyllen*, 399.

The gen. sing. ends in *-es*; *lyues*, 162; *doweþes*, 177. But cf. *fader*, 309, 428 (A.S. *fæder*).

Plurals.   The pl. usually ends in *-es*; as *þeynes*, 2; *biscopes*, 3; *eorles*, 5; *knyhtes*, 6; *þinges*, 30; *wordes*, 35; &c.

But also in *-en*; as *iwriten*, 103, 109 (cf. *writen*, pl., in Layamon, 9131); *blissen*, 50 (as in Layamon, 9027). In l. 77, *deden* is the dat. pl. (A.S. *dǣdum*); but Layamon has *deden* as nom. pl., l. 4864.

The following end in *-e*; *leode*, 27, 40, 212, from A.S. *lēod*, fem.; *saule*, 33 (A.S. *sāwla*, pl.); *wene*, 114 (A.S. *wēna*, pl.); *custe*, 252 (A.S. *cysta*, pl.); *ayhte*, 382 (A.S. *ǣhta*, pl.). But *ayhte* is also used in the singular, 185; spelt *eyhte*, 220. See *ǣhte* in Stratmann.

Genitives plural: *Englene*, 11; *monne*, 51; *ildre*, 185; *worde*, 418, where *vale worde*, answers to the A.S. *fela worda*, lit. 'few of words'.   In l. 419, *worde* is dat. pl.; see Layamon, 6675, 23632.   In l. 336, *quene* is probably a gen. pl., though it might be a gen. sing.[1]   The following are also plural forms: *ifon*, 191; *ivo*, 274; *freond*, 38.

§ 22. Adjectives.   The following end in *-e*, and are dissyllabic: *riche*, 56 (A.S. *rīce*); *wone*, 57 (see A.S. *wana*, adj., in Toller; it cannot always be a sb., as in Stratmann, s. v. *wane*); *schene*, 310; *vnlede*, 337; *stille*, 424.

Definite forms: nom. *þe erewe*, 236; dat. *þan arewe*, 228. *Nexte*, 371, is a weak superlative.   So is *þe wysuste*, 23.

Genitives singular: *longes*, 162; *vyches*, 384; *manyes*, 413.

Datives singular feminine: *owere*, 85; *echere*, 241; neuter, *reade*, 124.

Accusatives singular masculine: *godne*, 75; *vuelne*, 330; *swikelne*, 356.   *Owe*, 167, 189, is merely a shortened form of *owen*, 'own.'

Plurals in *-e*; *monye*, 2; *fele*, 3, 4; *þrute*, 5; *egleche*, 6

---

[1] The Icel. form of the proverb is:—'köld eru opt kvenna-rāð'; where *kvenna* is the gen. *plural*.

(sing. the same); *wyse*, 35; *i-sene*, 115 (sing. the same); *wroþe*, 115; *feye*, 170; *nenne*, 414.

Vocative plural: *leoue*, 38.

§ 23. Pronouns. *Ich*, I, 37, 214; dat. and acc. *me*; acc. pl. *vs*, 194. *þu*, thou, 196; dat. and acc. *þe*; pl. *ye*, 14; acc. *ou*, 29, *eu*, 214. Cf. *vre*, our, 42; *vre alre*, of us all, 96; *eure*, your, 28, 33; *ower*, your, 213. *He*, he, 13; dat. *him*, 57; acc. *hine*, 43, 59; *hyne*, 219. *Heo*, she, 251; dat. *hire*; acc. *hi*, 341. *Hit*, it, 145. *Hi*, they, 15, 117; *heo*, 116; acc. *heom*, them, 13. *Mi*, my, 27; *þire*, dat. f., thy, 243; *hire*, her, 249; *heore*, their, 15. *Þis*, this. Def. article: nom. masc. *þe*, 7; nom. neut. *þat*, 89; gen. masc. *þes*, 97; dat. masc. *þan*, 87, 228; dat. fem. *þare*, 8, 316; acc. masc. *þene*, 172, 290; *þane*, 350, 352; pl. acc. masc. *þas*, 170. This shows that traces of grammatical gender still lingered; we find that *time* (172) and *vnþeu* (290) are still masculine, *lawe* (8) and *neod* (316) are still feminine, and *land* (89) is neuter.

We may also notice the use of *me* for the indeterminate pronoun, like modern E. 'one', 347; *þe* is a relative, as in A.S., 100; and *o* is used as the indefinite article, 121. But the remarkable dual form *unc*, 'us two,' occurs only in the B-text, l. 583.

§ 24. Verbs. Infinitives end in *-en* or *-yen*; *-e* or *-ie* (*-ye*); or *-y*. As *lusten*, 28; *somnen*, 34; *libben*, 203; *howyen*, 135; cf. *beon*, 104, 300. Also *lere*, 13; *ileste*, 225; *iwurþe*, 263; *wurþie*, 60; *lokie*, 70; *wyssye*, 29; *vordrye*, 326; *arixlye*, 453; *leorny*, 107; *weny*, 345; cf. *beo*, 57. The verbs in *-ie*, *-ye*, *-y*, answer to the A.S. weak verbs in *-ian*; as *wurþie*, A.S. *wyrðian*. *Weny* suggests a fuller form *wēnian*, but the usual A.S. form is *wēnan*.

Gerunds: *to fone*, 88; *to werie*, 89; *to buwe*, 294; *to telle*, 416; all ending in *-e*. Also *to leden*, 76.

Present tense. 1 p. s. *munye* (weak verb), 37; 2 p. s. *yefst*, 182; *weldest*, 182; *hafst*, 198; *hauest*, 227; *lest* (lettest), 437; 3 p. s. *iburep*, 75; *bihouep*, 87; *flowep*, 146; and others ending in *-ep*. Also 3 p. s. *iwinp*, 151; *gop*, 217; *let* (lets), 298; *bihat*, 347; *dep* (doth), 406; *fop*, 407; *bip* (as future), 444. 1 p. pl. *wurchep*, 398; 3 p. pl. *beop*, 117.

Past tense. Strong: 3 p. s. *bigon*, 13; *quep*, 25. Past tense forms with present sense: *schal*, 57; *may*, 63; *not*, 172; *con*, 232; *wot*, 236; *on*, 240, 242; *parf*, 345. Cf. *pu myht*, 369, 377. Weak: 3 p. s. *luuede*, 20; *wolde*, 29; 3 p. pl. *sete*, 2; *scholden*, 16.

Subjunctive mood. Present: 3 p. s. *kunne*, 68; *habbe*, 91; *beo*, 92; *fare*, 98; *iqueme*, 156; *quele*, 156; *mvwe*, 170; &c. 2 p. pl. *mawe*, 14; *adrede*, 41. Past: *ahte*, 121; *hadde*, 123; *greowe*, 125; *wiste*, 266; *iseye*, 273.

Imperative. 2 p. s. *wurp*, 269; *chid*, 412; *ler*, 432. With the pron. *pu*, we find: *ne ilef pu*, 196; *ne seye pu*, 228; *ne gabbe pu*, 411. Also: *pu pe wune*, 367; *pu pe iwurche*, 374; *pu ne bigynne*, 415 (which is a subjunctive form).

Present participle: *uexynde*, 168; *singinde*, 230; *lyuyinde*, 278; *wexynde*, 433.

Past participle. Strong: *i-dryue*, 95; *biswike*, 116; *aswunde*, 117; *isowen*, 123; *ischapen*, 143; *ischote*, 421. Weak: *ilered*, 66; *ihurd*, 300; *i-sed*, 329; *i-seyd*, 335.

§ 25. Adverbs. These end in *-e*; as *swipe*, 8; *one*, 45; *yeorne*, 101; *lude and stille*, 325, 439; *vayre*, 347; &c.

§ 26. Prepositions. Usually with a dative case: as *a* (for *on*), 169; *after*, 141, 142; *from*, 367; *myd*, 77, 124, 322; *of*, 129; *on*, 126, 395; *ouer*, 48, 50; *to*, 202, 385, 397; *vpen, vppe, vppen*, 183, 197, 262; *wip*, 376, 412; *wypute*, 119, 241. *On* occurs after its case; 24.

With the accusative: *purh*, 363; *vnder*, 75.

With either acc. or dat.: *buuen*, 436.

For occurs with the dative, 250; but usually with the accusative, 204, 206, 278, 323.

§ 27. **Grammar of the B-text.** The preceding sketch of some of the grammatical details of the A-text is a sufficient guide to the grammatical forms of the B-text also. Both texts belong to the same dialect, and in a great number of instances employ the same suffixes, but with one remarkable variation. This is, that the scribe of the B-text, not always, but frequently, substitutes *i* for *e* in such suffixes; so that, in place of *-en, -es, -est, -eth*, he employs *-in, -is, -ist, -ith* or *-it*. Examples abound; as *lerin*, 13, *iherin*, 14, *sulin*, 16, &c.; *kinhis*, 2, *biscopis*, 3, *Godis*, 20, &c.; *wisiste*, 23, *mildist*, 52; *souit* (for *sowith*), 82; *cherricd* (for *cherrið*), 85, &c. So also *lerid* for *lered*, 66; &c. Yet we find several examples to the contrary; as *holden*, 72, *leden*, 76, &c.; *herles*, 5, *cnites*, 6, &c.; *hauest*, 181; *hauedest*, 448; *þenket* (for *þenketh*), 60. This shows, clearly enough, that this use of *i* for *e* is a personal matter, and must be disregarded as constituting an original feature. With this exception, the real peculiarities of the B-text are slight. The following may be noted :—

Substantives pl. in *-en* : *leden*, 27; *sawen*, 35; *dedin* (dat.), 77; *spechen*, 352; *honden*, 365; *heren*, 494; *neden* (dat.), 504. Cf. *bothen* (for *bothe*), 512. It may be observed that plural substantives in *-en* are rather common in the earlier text of Layamon, which even has *cnihten, goden*, for *cnihtes, godes*.

Amongst the pronominal forms we may notice : *ʒu*, you (acc.), 29; *ʒure*, your, 33; *he*, she, 262, 289; *hue*, she, 273; *hie*, she, 293; *hire*, her (acc.; where A has *hi*), 275, 341; *hem*, them, 13. The remarkable form *unc* appears, as the dual of the first personal pronoun, 583. As to the definite article, we may note the dat. fem. *þer*, 126; and the acc. masc. *þen*, 365, 627; badly written *þin*, 245. The word 'that' appears as *þet*, 143, 246.   The form *þines*, 500, should be *þine*.

Amongst the verbal forms we may note : *ard* (for *art*, thou art), 589 ; *arren* (are), 582 ; *ginne* (for *gin*, begin, imp.), 594-6 ; *wen* (for *went*, pr. s., goes), 221 ; *lat* (lets), 298 ; *bihait* (promises), 347 ; *deʒh* (pr. s. avails, is good), 506 ; *þarf* (pr. s. need, needs), 461 ; *duʒen* (pr. pl. avail), 546.

The use of *bes* for *best* (thou shalt be) 509, is probably an error ; the better form *best* occurs in 558.   Similarly, *hwendes*, 569, should be *wendest* ; cf. *hauest*, 181.   So also *les*, 437, is for *lest*, a contracted form of *lettest* ; cf. *weldest* just above, 430.   And I would explain *bus*, 621, as short for *bust* (lit. bowest, but used as a future, ' shalt bow ') ; see note.   The present participles are *singende*, 230 ; *liuihinde*, 278 ; *desiende*, 466 ; *lusninde*, 646.   Cf. l. 474.

Two words are run into one in *letet* (*let it*, let it go, neglect it), 525 ; *tellit* (tell it), 669 ; *shaltu* (shalt thou), 358 ; *wurþu* (be thou), 269 ; *wose* (who so), 298 ; *ate* (at the), 372 ; *aten* (at the), 570.   Cf. note to l. 318.

After a *t*, an initial þ sometimes becomes *t*; as in *þat ti*, 232 ; but not in the next line, because *þe* is emphatic, meaning ' thee ' ; *it te*, 524, where *te* likewise means ' thee ', but is unstressed, as again in *miht te*, 648.   Similarly, þ once becomes *t* after *and*, as in *and te*, 236.

§ 28. Metre of the Poem.   The metre is very irregular. The following remarks upon it are taken from ten Brink's Early English Literature, English Version (1883), p. 152. ' The metrical form in which these Proverbs of Ælfred are clothed is of moment.   In them we find the ancient long line in the midst of its transformation into the short couplet. Alliteration, imperfectly carried out and often too lavishly employed, alternates with or accompanies rime, which, like the alliteration, connects the two halves of a long line.

(*Footnote*): As a matter of course, the rime is more consistently used, the alliteration more deranged, in some Proverbs than in others.   The former are not necessarily older than the latter on this account.—But the rime falls upon the final syllables of the members of the line which it binds ; further, unlike the alliteration, it can make no difference between the first and second half-line ; hence it makes us feel that what it joins is dual, is a pair.   The following seems clearly a unit :—

*w*it and *w*isdom : and i*w*riten reden (A 102–3),

and in spite of the massing of alliteration, the following is also felt to be a unit :—

He wes *w*is on his *w*ord : and *w*ar on his *w*erke (A 21–2).

But in the line—

He wes king, and he wes *clerk* : wel he luuede godes *werk*
    (A 19, 20)—

we perceive a riming couplet, and the alliteration, confined to the short line (*k*ing, *c*lerk—*w*el, *w*erk) seems merely an ornament.

'We noted the same, or similar peculiarities of form in a few poems of the eleventh century, especially in the song on Ætheling Ælfred (A.S. Chronicle, an. 1036). If we place later products side by side with them, we are compelled to conclude that the popular poetry of the twelfth century, so far as it was original, ranged chiefly within such forms as these.'

§ 29. **Varieties of metre.** I here follow, in the main, the account of the Metre of this poem given by Dr. Schipper in his Englische Metrik (Bonn, 1882), ch. 7 ; pp. 146–62. He remarks that we find here *four* distinct varieties of versification. Taking two short lines to constitute one long line, the four varieties are these :—

1. Alliterating long lines that observe, more or less strictly, the old metrical rules.

2. Lines that exhibit both alliteration and rime, or else alliteration and assonance or half-rime.

3. Lines devoid of alliteration, but exhibiting either rime or assonance.

4. Lines that merely exhibit four strongly stressed syllables, but devoid of alliteration or rime.

Examples of such lines will now be given.

§ 30. 1. **Alliterating lines.**   (All the examples are from Text A.)   These are of four kinds.

(*a*) Lines in which the alliteration is correctly employed, i.e. with *two* alliterating syllables in the former half of the line, and *one* in the latter.

> he ou *w*ólde *w*ýssye : *w*ísliche þínges (29).
> .*M*íldeliche ich *m*únye : *m*ýne leo·ue¹ fréond (37).
> *B*úte-if he *b*éo : in *b*óke i-léred (65).
> *w*ít and *w*ísdom : and i-*w*ríten réden (102).
> and þat *g*óld *g*réowe : so *g*rés doþ· on éorþe (125).

(*b*) Lines with *one* alliterating syllable in the former half, and *two* in the latter.

> wólde ye, mi *l*éode : *l*ústen eu·re *l*óuerde (27).
> hw· ye mýhte *w*órldes : *w*úrþshipes *w*élde (31).
> he· is óne *m*ónne : *m*íldest *m*áyster (51).

So also 53, 384, 386, 437.

(*c*) Lines with only *two* alliterating syllables (these are numerous).

> þús queþ *A*lured : *é*nglene fróuer (25).
> and ék eure *s*áule : *s*ómnen to Críste (33).

So also 41, 45, 47, 49, 55, 57, 67, &c.

---

¹ The dot in 'leo·ue' indicates that the *eo* receives a secondary stress. Many of the lines contain syllables of this character.

(*d*) Lines with *four* such syllables.

He wes *wí*s on his *wó*rd : and *wá*r on his *wé*rke (21).
*lú*uyen hin' and *lý*kyen : for he· is *ló*uerd of *lý*f (43).

§ 31. 2. (*a*) Lines with alliteration and rime.

þe *éo*rl and· þe *é*þelý*ng* : ibúreþ un·der gō·dne kí*ng* (74).
þat *ló*nd to *lé*den : mid *lá*welich·e dé*den* (76).
þat þe *ch*írche ha·bbe grý*þ* : and þe *ch*éorl beo· in frý*þ* (91).
his *sé*des to· *só*wen : his *mé*des to· *mó*wen (93).
þenne béoþ his *wé*ne : ful *wró*þe i-sé*ne* (114).

(*b*) Lines with alliteration and assonance (i.e. vowel-rime
only).

*Á*lured, he wes· in *é*ngle ló*nd* : and kí*ng*, wel swíþe stró*ng* (17).
hwych *só* þe mon *só*weþ : al *s*wúch he schal mó*we* (82).
þan *kn*ýhte bi-hó*ueþ* : *k*énlich' on· to fó*ne* (87).
hym-séolue for-*yé*meþ : for-*yé*teþ̄ and· for-l*é*seþ (207).

(*c*) Lines with alliteration and half-rime (consonantal
rime).

íf þu háuest *sé*o*rewe* : ne *sé*ye þu hít þan á*rewe* (227).
þéyh heo *wé*l *wó*lde : ne máy heo hi nówiht *wé*lde (283).
ac íf þu hím lest *wé*lde : *wé*xende· on *wó*rlde (437).

§ 32. 3. (*a*) Lines with rime only.

þe *pó*ure and· þe *rý*che : démen i lý*che* (80).
*yó*uþ' and al· þat he háv'þ i-dró*we* : is þen·ne wél bi-tó*we* (157).
ne *nó* mon þe·ne é*nde* : hwenn' he· schal héonne wé*nde* (174).
*mó*nymo·n sí*ngeþ* : þat wíf ho·m brí*ngeþ* (264).
and *ó*fte þa·t *wó*lde : dó þat heo· ne schó*lde* (288).

(*b*) Lines with assonance only.

þénne cum·eþ é*lde* : á*nd* unhé*lþe* (112). (*Read* and ék unhé*lþe*.)
and he hí hadd' i-só*wen* : á*lle* myd réade gó*lde* (123).
byfó*re* he· þe mé*neþ* : byhýnde he· þe té*leþ* (237).

(*c*) Lines with half-rime only.

héom he gon· lé*re* : *s*ó ye máw' i-hú*re* (13).
for hwát is gó*ld* bu·te stó*n* : but·íf hit háueþ wí·s mó*n* (131).
néuer upon éo*rbe* : to wló*n*k þu n'ywú*rþe* (183).

§ 33. 4. Lines with neither rime nor alliteration; but only four strongly stressed syllables.

éorles prúte : knýhtes egléche (5).
póure and ríche : léode mýne (39).
he may béon on élde : wénliche lórþeu (104).
ne scólde neu'er yóng mon : hówyen to swíþe (134).
wélden u're mádmes : and léten us byhínde (193).
sérewe if' þu háuest : and þ'érewe hit wót (235).

It may be remarked that the mixture of alliteration with occasional riming greatly tended to disturb the number of stressed syllables in a line. For whereas the former only required *four* strongly stressed syllables in the complete line, the latter really required *six* to give it its true *dual* character, as in lines 174–5 ; see § 32 (*a*). Indeed, we can hardly scan lines 157–8 without introducing as many as *seven* such syllables. It must be felt that this unfortunate uncertainty as to what may be at any time expected is extremely disconcerting to a reader accustomed only to modern methods of prosody. It is hardly profitable to examine each line in still closer detail ; it may suffice to say that Layamon's Brut is written in a similarly fluctuating metre.

§ 34. In order to show the general effect of the metre in consecutive lines, I follow Dr. Schipper in quoting the third section (lines 61–72).

þús queþ *Á*lfred : *é*nglene uróuer,
Ne may' non ríhtwis *k*íng : ben un'der *Cr*íste séoluen
*b*út' if he *b*éo : in *b*óke i-léred,
and hé his *w*rítes : swíþe *w*el' kúnne ;
and he cúnne *l*éttres : *l*óki' him-seolf' óne,
*h*ú he schul' his *l*ónd : *l*áweli'che *h*ólde.

§ 35. **The Dialect of the Poem.** It is needless to say much on this point, as the grammatical details given in §§ 21–27 are sufficient to show that the texts are throughout in the

Southern dialect. The metre points in the same direction, as it much resembles that employed in Layamon's Brut. Perhaps it is worth while to repeat here that such a form as *wendes* (569) is a mere error of a Norman scribe for *wendest*, and not an example of a Northern suffix.

§ 36. **Date of the Poem.** The indications all point to a very early date. The Jesus College MS. itself is of the thirteenth century. Dr. Morris (Pref. to O.E. Misc., p. xi) suggests that one of the poems in it was composed about 1244. I think it is worth while to say that one of the lines in that poem, viz. 'The archebisscop Stephne for hire [i. e. the church] gon to fyhte,' l. 22, must surely refer to the famous Stephen Langton, archbishop of Canterbury from 1207 to 1228; and seems to show that the said poem is at any rate later than 1228. If, however, it be admitted that the majority of the poems in the Jesus College MS. were composed about 1250, it at once becomes plain that at least three of the poems which it contains are conspicuously of a still earlier date, viz. The Bestiary, the Proverbs of Alfred, and the Moral Ode; not considering The Owl and the Nightingale, which is not included in The Old English Miscellany, and need not be here discussed. I think there can be no question that The Proverbs of Alfred really belong to the former half of the thirteenth century. The testimony of the Trinity MS. is even stronger. It has been said to be 'of the beginning of the thirteenth century' (p. vii); and the curious way in which the scribe tries to reproduce the A.S. characters, especially that for *w*, shows that it was written at a time when that character was still regarded as essential. And as to the lost Cotton MS., it is remarkable that not only does Wanley, in his extract, print it altogether in A.S. characters, but the transcript in MS. James 6 is marked by the same peculiarity. If the Cotton MS. really employed the A.S. characters, not for *w* only, but for such letters as *r*, *s*, and *f*, it must obviously have been written out at a fairly early date. Wanley's opinion as to this question is explicit; he describes it as 'litteris Normanno-Saxonicis circa temp. Henrici II. aut Richardi I. conscriptum', i. e. before 1200.

The expression in l. 11, 'Englenes durling,' may well have been taken from Layamon's Brut, where (as I show in the Note) such an expression occurs eight times (cf. Note to l. 4); and I think we ought to lay stress on ll. 570-2, where Part II of the poem concludes with the remark—'say thou, *at the end*, "happen what may, God's will be done"'; for it is the fact that this is precisely the phrase with which Layamon had concluded his work. If we date the Brut about A.D. 1205, I see no reason why we may not date these 'Proverbs' between A.D. 1205 and 1210.

§ 37. Opinion of ten Brink. I can hardly do better than reproduce here the judicious account given by ten Brink, in his Early English Literature (p. 151 of the English version).

' Many a memory from the more ancient period of its history may still have been living among the English people in the twelfth century. But above all shone forth the image of king Ælfred, that had descended from father to son as a precious heirloom. Single features had been impaired, and some new traits added, but in the main it was like the original: the ruler who loved his subjects as did no other, the man of power and gentleness, who was at once king, father, and teacher of his people.

'From this latter office, Ælfred came gradually to be regarded as a source of popular wisdom. A number of proverbs and maxims were ascribed to him.

' There existed, in the twelfth century, collections of gnomic poems with the title Proverbs (Parabolæ) or Precepts (Documenta) of Ælfred. These were given to posterity in several versions, varying in compass, arrangement, and (partly) in contents.

'A few[1] recensions from the thirteenth century are preserved; the existence of others is proved by citations in a contemporary poem.[2] Three distinct parts have recently been pointed out in the more complete text; though it is still doubtful if they really owe their origin to three different epochs, since ancient and modern matters are intermingled within the compass of shorter sections.'

§ 38. **The three Parts.** It was pointed out by Wülker (see p. 9 of Gropp's dissertation) that the work may be divided into three Parts. The first Part is contained in ll. 1–210, and consists of a prologue (1–24), an exordium (25–60), and ten proverbs (61–210), each of which is quoted as being a saying of Alfred. The second Part is contained in ll. 211–572, and consists of an exordium (211–25), and sixteen proverbs or sayings of Alfred (226–572) of which the Jesus College MS. contains ten only. The third Part is slightly different in character, as each section of the part begins with the same words, viz. 'Sone min so leue,' or 'Sone min so dere,' or 'Leue sone dere,' the advice being addressed to Alfred's son only; it consists of an exordium (573–605), and four pieces of advice (606–709), the last section of all being capable of subdivision into three parts. None of this third Part is extant in the briefer Text, and it may be regarded as a supplement; but it is idle to make much of this. The speculations that are quoted by Gropp as founded upon this circumstance, and the question as to alleged 'interpolations', are hardly worth considering; guesses of this kind can be

[1] Only two; how many others there may have been is unknown.
[2] I.e. in The Owl and the Nightingale, in which several proverbs are cited. Some of them are expressly attributed to 'Alfred king', whose name occurs in ll. 235, 294, 299, 349, 685, 697, 761, 942, 1074, 223, 1269.

made by anybody, and usually convince nobody. It is sufficient to observe that ll. 644-5 are repeated at ll. 661-2 and ll. 678-9, and that, from l. 644 onward, riming couplets are more frequent. From l. 661 to the end we have such couplets only, though just a few of the rimes are mere assonances. And although words of French origin are extremely scarce throughout the rest of the poem, we actually find *four* such words close together, in the last three lines.

On the other hand, the presumably early Cotton MS. quotes lines 652 and 653, which looks as if the greater portion of Part III is nearly as old as all that precedes it. On the whole there is just a presumption that ll. 660-709 were added by the latest compiler of the material, or shortly before his time.

§ 39. **The subject.** The subject of early popular Proverbs is one upon which a whole book may easily be written; but this is not, in my opinion, the place for considering it. I have pointed out some of the more important references in the Notes on the Proverbs appended (at p. 71) to the Notes on the Text; and the student will find much upon the subject in Kemble's edition of the Dialogue of Salomon and Saturnus, where the Proverbs of Alfred (Text B) and the Proverbs of Hendyng are given at length, and the requisite passages from the Owl and the Nightingale are duly collected. When we notice that the eleven proverbs attributed to Alfred in that poem nearly all of them differ from those in the Poem here printed, it becomes clear that it was just then the fashion to attribute all proverbs to Alfred; a consideration which explains the whole matter.

I add here, for the reader's convenience, the more important of the remarks or references given in Gropp's dissertation.

§ 40. **Gropp's dissertation.** Gropp had access to Spelman's Life of King Alfred, which he sometimes quotes. At p. 12, he refers to the Dialogue of Salomon and Saturnus, but it throws very little light upon our poem; also to A Father's Instructions to his Son, in the Exeter Book, called by Grein 'Fæder Lārcwidas'. The latter has some similarity to sections 30–3. With respect to Alfred's love of proverbs, he quotes from 'Alfred de Rievaux', i.e. Ailred (Æthelred) de Rievaulx, as follows: 'Extant parabolæ ejus plurimum habentes aedificationis, sed et venustatis et jucunditatis. Leges christianissimas et scripsit et promulgavit, in quibus fides ejus et devotio in Deum, sollicitudo in subditos, misericordia in pauperes, justitia circa omnes cunctis legentibus patet.' And again, from the Chronica Wintoniensis: 'In proverbiis ita enituit, ut nemo post illum amplius.' From Asser's Life of Alfred he quotes the passage which relates how the king kept a book in which to enter useful quotations, which he called his Enchiridion or Manual, because he carefully kept it always at hand; cf. Six Old English Chronicles, in Bohn's Series, p. 77.

At p. 15 of Gropp's essay occurs the following passage, which Wülker quotes in his Grundriss der angelsächsischen Litteratur, p. 437 :—'The chief contents of the book [i. e. Ælfred's Manual] must have been this collection of wise sentences which he took from the Holy Scripture and from the other writers he read with Asser. Now, as the King according to Asser's testimony, eagerly desired to teach others, it is not impossible that he should have communicated the wise maxims thus gained to his people by composing a particular versified collection of Proverbs for this purpose.... It is possible that there may be some relation between the first part [of the present work, ll. 1–210] and king Ælfred; for many thoughts expressed in it may be found in his other works, chiefly in his translation of Boethius De Consolatione Philosophiæ'.[1] Upon which Wülker remarks that Gropp does not explain whether 'The Proverbs' were taken partly from the Manual and partly from Boethius, or whether select passages were copied from Boethius into the Manual. I am afraid that it is all guesswork, and likely to remain so.[2]

At pp. 17–20, Gropp has some 'Metrical Observations', in which he agrees with Schipper ; see § 29.

At pp. 21–39, he analyses the vowels and consonants employed in the MSS.; at pp. 39–52, the grammatical inflexions ; and at p. 53, considers the foreign element.

Words of Latin origin are *bishop, clerk, siker, turn* (A.S. *biscop, clerc, sicor, tyrnan*). Words of French origin :— *poure*, 39, 375, *mayster*, 52, 299, 685, *lettres*, 69, *trayen* (in comp. *to-trayen*), 303, *couere*, 342 (*coueren*, B. 595), *kache* (in comp. *bi-kache*), 359, *armes*, 649, *stable*, 673, *multeplien*, 675, *huge*, 697, 709, *gentile*, 707, *gentileri*, 708, *amendith*, 709, *companie*, 709. Perhaps also *prute*, 5, *pruden*, 686.

French words of Teutonic origin are :—*scarneth* (B. 238); *orgul* (in comp. *orgul-prute*), 286 ; *i-hasted* (B. 255). Also *gyle*, 328, 664. The exact origin of *wilis*, 649, *gyle*, 328, 664, and *bi-wilen*, B. 328, is still somewhat obscure.

As might be expected in a piece which so wholly belongs to the Southern dialect, the Norse influence is very slight. We may notice *fro* (in *ther-fro*), B. 188, *scumes*, 334, *lythinges*, 416, *tresten*, 505, *costes*, 535, *ille*, 652.

The rest of Gropp's dissertation (pp. 54–61) is occupied with Notes upon the readings of the text, all of which I have

---

[1] Wülker does not complete the sentence, which thus concludes :— 'as for instance, those about the futility of earthly wealth, the highest good, the duty of the wise man to be content with his fate.'

[2] We only know that eleven proverbs are cited as Alfred's in The Owl and the Nightingale ; and that none of them exactly agrees with any of the Proverbs of Alfred !

consulted. Corrections of his which are certainly right are : *seluen* for *selues*, B. 64; omit *Wid*, B. 119; *vurþere* for *wrþere*, B. 128; *fremede* (or *fremde*) for *frumþe*, 129 ; read *ouer-goð*, B. 217; read *wraþed*, B. 276; read *for-swunken*,[1] B. 292 ; read *i-wraþed*, B. 320; read *i-selþe*, 362 ; read *leʒen*, B. 368 ; read *londe*, 379 ; read *hwile he in þis werld beþ*, B. 407 ; read *duʒeþe*, 516; *senden* [of course he means *sende*] represents the 3 p. s. subj. pres. of *senden*, to send, 517 ; *letet=let it*, 525 ; *funden*=seek, tend, depart, 553 ; *beuir*=trembling, adj., 627 ; read *liʒen*, 'lie,' 670 ; *sug*='such,' 676 ; with *leþe-bei* in 692, compare *leoðe-beie* in Stratmann.

§ 41. Literature of the subject.

EDITIONS. (1) By T. Wright (1841); in Reliquiæ Antiquæ, ed. Wright and Halliwell; see § 2. (2) By J. M. Kemble (1848); in Salomon and Saturnus; see § 3. (3) By R. Morris (1872); in An Old English Miscellany; see § 4.

EXTRACTS. (1) R. Morris, Specimens of Early English ; by the Rev. Richard Morris, LL.D. Part I. Oxford, 1882. At p. 146 an extract is given from Text A, including ll. 1–60, 73–85, 159–79, 195–210, 227–46, 410–56. At p. 329 there are a few notes; and some of the words are explained in the Glossarial Index. (2) The same; a second edition, revised by myself, 1885. Some new notes were added, and the glossary revised. (3) Alt- und mittelenglisches Übungsbuch, mit einem Wörterbuche von J. Zupitza ; siebente verbesserte Auflage bearbeitet von J. Schipper. Wien und Leipzig; 1904. At pp. 102–3 there is a short extract, viz. ll. 73–98 ; from both Texts.

REMARKS. Über die Neuangelsächsischen Sprüche des König Ælfred; by Dr. R. Wülker. In Paul und Braune's Beiträge, vol. i. p. 243 (1873).

---

[1] But he wrongly explains *for swunken* by saying that *swunken* is the dative plural of O.E. *swinc* !

On the Language of The Proverbs of Alfred; by E. Gropp. Halis Saxonum; MDCCCXXIX (*sic*)[1]. A dissertation, written in English; pp. 1–61. A useful piece of work, which I have duly considered; there are critical notes, pp. 54–61, some of which I have adopted. The author had not the advantage of knowing the true readings of the Trinity MS.; nor had he any knowledge of the James MS. Considering that this dissertation was written as long ago as 1879, it is very well done. But we must not attach weight to remarks which the new evidence and our better knowledge of Middle-English at the present date have necessarily rendered obsolete. See further above, in § 40.

Note by J. Zupitza; in Anglia, iii. 370 (1880). He quotes, on the authority of Dr. Christoph Walther, a curious inscription, dated 1575, over a fireplace in a room belonging to the Rathskeller at Lübeck, as follows:—

> Mennich man lude synghet,
> Wen men em de brut bringet:
> Weste he, wat men em brochte,
> Dat he wol wenen mochte.

Which I roughly translate thus:—

> Many a man full loudly sings
> When his bride he homeward brings
> Wist he, what he home had led,
> He well might weep and wail instead.

The resemblance to ll. 264–7 of our poem is so close that Herr Walther conjectures that the saying may have been imported from the Steelyard in London. We must remember that the lines recur in the later Proverbs of Hending, ll. 133–8; ed. Böddeker.

Englische Metrik; von Dr. J. Schipper. Erster Theil;

---

[1] A singular error; read MDCCCLXXIX, as the facts require. The author was born in 1854.

Bonn, 1882. In chapter 7, the metre of the Proverbs is clearly explained, and compared with that of Layamon's Brut.

The Proverbs of Alfred; by the Rev. Prof. Skeat. In the Transactions of the Philological Society, 1895-8; pp. 399-418. I here discuss and explain the spelling of the Trinity MS., and give the results of a collation of Wright's text with the same at pp. 416-18. See § 6.

The student who desires further information on the subject of proverbs generally, may consult English Proverbs and Proverbial Phrases, by W. Carew Hazlitt, London, 1869; the collection of medieval proverbs by Müllenhof and Scherer, specimens of which are given in Die älteste deutsche Litteratur, by Prof. Dr. Paul Piper, Berlin and Stuttgart (1884); pp. 275-85; and the collections referred to by Kemble. A good general collection is that by Ida von Düringsfeld, entitled Sprichwörter der Germanischen und Romanischen Sprachen; 2 vols. 1872-5. I give numerous references to this book on pp. 71-3.

My thanks are especially due to Professor Dr. W. Heuser, of Göttingen, for his assistance with regard to the James MS., as explained in § 15; to Mr. F. Madan, of the Bodleian Library, for valuable information concerning it; and to Professor Napier, Litt.D., of Oxford, for his kindness in collating my proof-sheets with the same MS.

CAMBRIDGE,
Dec. 24, 1906.

THE PROVERBS OF ALFRED

The Text is exhibited in three forms, as follows :—

A. The shorter text, as in the Jesus College (Oxford) MS. no. 29 ; lines 1–456. Printed on the left-hand pages, as far as p. 40.

B. The longer text, as in the Trinity College (Cambridge) MS. B. 14. 39 ; lines 1–709. Printed on the right-hand pages, as far as p. 41 ; and afterwards upon both pages.

C. Fragments of a third text, as formerly extant in MS. Cotton, Galba A. xix, but now only preserved in three imperfect copies. Printed in the lower part of pages 2–13, as far as l. 98 ; after which only variations from Text B are recorded, all from MS. J.

Of the three copies, W. denotes that by Wanley (lines 1–30); S. denotes that by Spelman (lines 1–98); and J. the fragmentary copy in MS. James 6.

Incipiunt documenta Regis Aluredi.

A. 1. (PART I.)

AT Seuorde
   séte þeynes monye,
fele Biscopes,
   and feole boc-iléred,   4
Eorles prute,
   knyhtes egleche.
Þar wes þe eorl Alurich,
   of þare lawe swiþe wis,   8
And ek Ealured,
   Englene hurde,
Englene durlyng;
   on Engle-londe he wes kyng.   12
Heom he bi-gon lére,
   so ye mawe i-hure,
hw hi heore lif
   lede scholden.   16

From Jesus Coll. MS. 29, leaf 189 (262); *denoted by* A.   12. A.
englene londe; *but see* l. 24.   13. *Read* gon (*for* bi-gon).

Alfredi conciones.

C. 1.   At Sifforde
      seten þeines manie,
fele biscopes,
   fele boc-lered,   4
Erles prude,
   and cnihtes egleche.
þer was Erl Alfrich,
   of þe lage swuðe wis,   8

W = Wanley's transcript; S = Spelman; J = James; ll. 1–30 *are from*
W.   6. ⁊ = and J; WS *omit.*   7. erle J.

B. 1. (PART I.)

At Siforde
   setin kingis monie,
fele biscopis,
   and fele booc-lerede,   **4**
erles prude,
   and cnihtes egleche;
þer *was* erl [Alfrich],
   of þe lawe suiþe wis,   **8**
and eke Alfred,
   Englene herde,
Englene derling;
   in Engelonde he was king.   **12**
Hem he gon lerin,
   so ȝe muȝen i-herin,
hu [hi hure] lif
   lede shuldin.   **16**

I give here the rejected spellings and misreadings of MS. B.   **2.**
kinhis.   **5.** herles.   **6.** cnites.   **7.** alfred (!).   **9.** heke.
12. enkelonde.   **14.** *we* (*error for* ȝe).   **15.** *whu we ȝure; read*
hu hi hure.   **16.** sulin.

---

   and ec Alfred,
      Engle hirde,
   Engle derling; .
      on Engelonde he was king.   **12**
   Hem he gan leren,
      swo hi heren mihten,
   hu hi here lif
      leden scolden.   **16**

  9. and SJ: W *omits.*   Alfred S; Alfrede WJ.   **11.** engla J.
12. Englond J.   **13.** leren JS; laren W.

Alured, he wes in Engle-lond,
　　and king, wel swiþe strong.
He wes king, and he wes clerk,
　　wel he luuede Godes werk.　　　　　　20
He wes wis on his word,
　　and war on his werke ;
he wes þe wysuste mon
　　þat wes Engle-londe on.　　　　　　　24

A. 2.

þvs queþ Alured,
　　Englene frouer :
' wolde ye, mi leode,
　　lusten éure louerde,　　　　　　　　28
he óu wolde wyssye
　　wisliche þinges,
hw ye myhte worldes
　　wurþshipes welde,　　　　　　　　　32

17. A. englene.　　　19. A. clerek.　　　32. A. wrþsipes.

'Alfred, he was on Engelond
　　a king wel swiðe strong ;
he was king and clerc,
　　wel he luuede Godes werc.　　　　　　20
he was wis on his worde,
　　and war on his speche ;
he was þe wiseste man
　　at was on Engelond[e].　　　　　　　24

21. *All* wise ; *see* l. 8.　　worde J ; word WS.　　22. war WS ; ware J.
23. wiseste JS ; wisest W.　　　　　　24. Engelond J ; Englond S ;
Engelond on W.

Alfred, he *was in* Engelonde a king,
   wel swiþe strong and lufsum þing.
He *was* king and clerc,
   ful *wel* he louede Godis werc.   2ɔ
He was wis *on* his word,
   and war *on* his werke;
he was þe wisiste mo*n*
• þat was *in* Engelonde on.   24

B. 2.

Þus q*u*ad Alfred,
   Englene frouere:
'*w*olde ʒe, mi leden,
   lustin ʒure louird,   28
and he ʒu *w*olde wissin
   of *w*i[s]liche þinges,
hu ʒe mihtin *in w*er*e*lde
   wurshipe *w*eldin,   3ɔ

17. Alfred *is superfluous*; enkelonde.   19. cleric.   24. þad;
see note.   26, 54. frowere; *but see* l. 62.   27. *we* (*for* ʒe);
mi *or* nu (*doubtful*).   29. *Perhaps omit* and.   31. ʒu *we* (*for*
wu ʒe, *i. e.* hu ʒe); miſtin; þ'elde.   32. wrsipe.

C. 2.   Ðus cwað Alured,
       Engle frofre:
'*w*olde ʒe nu liþen
   and lusten ʒure louerd,   28
and he ʒu wolde wisen
   wisliche þinges,
hu ʒe mihten werldes
   wurðscipe welden,   32

30. wisliche WJ; wiseliche S. *Here* W *ends.*   31. werldes J;
werlds S.   32. wurðscipe J; wurthe cipe S.

and ek eure saule
  somnen to Criste.'
Wyse were þe wordes
  þe seyde þe king Alured: 36
' Mildeliche ich munye,
  myne leoue freond,
poure and riche,
  leode myne,   40
þat ye alle a-drede
  vre dryhten Crist,
luuyen hine and lykyen;
  for he is louerd of lyf.   44
He is one god
  ouer alle godnesse;
He is one gleaw
  ouer alle glednesse;   48
He is one blisse
  ouer alle blissen.
He is one monne
  mildest mayster;   52

---

and ec ȝure soule
  samne to Criste.'
Wise weren þe cweþen
  þe saide þe king Alfred: 36
' Mildeliche I mune ȝu,
  mine dere frend,
arme and edi[e],
  lede luuiende,   40
þat ȝe alle dreden
  ȝure drihten Crist,

35-40. J *omits.* 35. cwethen S. 37. yu S. 39, 40. edilede (*sic*) S.
41. J *om.* þat ȝe. Alle dreden J; all dred S. 42. criste J; christ S.

and eke ȝure saulle
  samne to Criste.'
*W*ise werin þe sawen
  of ki*n*g Alfred :   36

   .   .   .   .

   .   .   .   .   .

'Arme and edie ledin,
  of liuis do*m* :   40
þat ȝe alle dredin
  ȝure drihtin Crist,
lovin him and likin ;
  for he is louird ouir lif.   44
He is one god
  ouer alle godnesse ;
and he is gleu
  ouer alle glade þinges ;   48
He is one blisse
  ouer alle blithnesse.
He is one mon[ne]
  mildist maist*er* ;   52

33. heke ; salle.   35. þis *or* wis ; *read* wise ; *see* A. *and* C.
36. ki*n*c.   41. þad *we*.   42. driftin.   48. þinhes.   50. blítnesse.
51. mon.

---

luuien him and liken ;
  for he is louerd of lif.   44
He is one god
  ouer all[e] godnesse . . .   46
He is one blisse   49
  ouer all[e] blessedness.
He is one manne
  milde master ;   52

43–62. J *omits.*   43. luviend S ; licen S.   44. loverd S.
45. God S.   46, 50. all S.

He is one folkes
    fader and frouer.
He is one rihtwis,
    and so riche king,   56
þat him ne schal beo wone
    nouht of his wille,
[hwo] hine her on worlde
    wurþie þencheþ.'   60

A. 3.

Þvs queþ Alured,
    Englene urouer:
' Ne may non ryhtwis king
    [ben] vnder Criste seoluen,   64
bute-if he beo
    in boke ilered,
and he his [writes]
    swiþe wel kunne,   68

59. A. we (*for* wo = hwo); *read* hwo (*see* B. *and* C.). 60. A. wrþie.
64. *Supply* ben ; *see* B. *and* C. 67. A. wyttes ; *read* writes ; *see* B. *and* C.

He [is] one folce
    fader and frofre;
he is one riht-wis,
    and [so] riche king,   56
þat him ne scal be wane
    noht of his will[e],
hwo him here on werld[e]
    wurðen ðenkeþ.'   60

53. S *omits* is. 55. riht-wise S. 56. S *omits* so. 57. pane
(*for* wane) S. 58. will S. 59. werld S. 60. wurthend and
eth (!) S ; *read* wurðen ðenkeþ.

He is one folkes
　　fadir and frouere.
He is one riht-wis,
　　and suo riche king,　　　　　　　　　　56
nat him shal ben wone
　　no-þing of his wille,
hƿo him her on ƿorulde
　　wurþin þenkeþ.'　　　　　　　　　　　60

B. 3.

Þus quad Alfred,
　　Englene frouere:
'May no riche king
　　ben onder Crist seluen,　　　　　　　64
bote-ȝif he be
　　booc-[i]lerid,
and [he] hi[s] ƿrites
　　ƿel [i]kenne,　　　　　　　　　　　68

54. frowere (*see* l. 62).　　55. riſte wis.　　57. *for* nat him *read* þat him ne.　　sal.　　58. is.　　59. ƿo.　　60. wrþin þenket.
64. selues (*against grammar; read* seluen).　　65. þif (*for* ȝif).
67. *I supply* he; hi (*close to the margin; s cut away*).

C. 3.　　Ðus cwaþ Alvred,
　　Engle frofre:
'Ne mai no riht cing
　　ben under Crist selfe,　　　　　　　64
bute he be boc-lered
　　and wis o loare,
and [him] hise writes
　　wel icweme,　　　　　　　　　　　68

61. cwath S.　　63–72. *Preserved in* J.　　63. Ne J; He S.
64. Crist selfe S; criste self J.　　65. bute J; but S.　　66. wis J; wise S.　　loare J; loage S.　　67. J *omits* and. *Both* he; *read* him.
hise writes S; is wittes J.　　68. *Both* icweme.

and he cunne lettres
lokie him-seolf one,
hw he schule his lond
laweliche holde.'   72

A. 4.

þus queþ Alured:
' þe eorl and þe eþelyng
ibureþ, vnder gódne king,
þat lond to leden   76
myd lawelyche deden.
And þe clerk and þe knyht
schulle démen euenliche riht;
þe poure and þe ryche   80
[hi schulle] démen ilyche.
Hwych so þe mon soweþ,
al swuch he schal mowe;
and eueruyches monnes dom   84
to his owere dure churreþ.'

78. A. clerek.   79. A. he schulle ; *omit* he; *see* l.81.   A. eueliche.
81. *I supply* hi schulle *from* l. 79, *where* A. *has* he schulle *by mistake.*

---

and he cunne lettres
locen himselfe,
hu he scal his lond
lageliche holden.'   72

C. 4.   Ðus cwaþ Alvred,
Engle frofre :   73*
' þe erl and þe aþeling,
þo ben under þe cing,

69. lettres J ; letres S.   71. scal S ; scall J.   72. lageliche J ;
lagelice S. *Both* helden.   73*. *In* S *only.*   74–83. *Preserved in* J.
74. erl J ; Earl S.

and bote he cunnie letteris
  lokin him-seluen,
hu he shule his lond
  laweliche holden.'   72

B. 4.

Þus quad Alfred:
' Þe erl and þe eþeling
  þo ben vnder þe king,
þe lond to leden   76
  mid laweliche dedin.
Boþe þe clerc and þe cniht
  demen euenliche riht.

      80

        .   .   .   .   .   .

For aftir þat mon sowiþ
  al suich shal he mowin;
and eueriches monnes dom   84
  to his oȝe dure cherriõ.'

71. wu (*for* hu); sule.   73. helfred.   74. herl; heþeling.
77. lauelichi.   78. cnit.   79. rict.   80, 81. *Not in* B.
82. souit.   83. alsuipich (!) sal; mouin.   85. cherricd (!).

þe lond to leden   76
  mid lageliche deden.
Boðe þe clerc and þe cniht
  demen euenliche riht . . .   79
For after þat te man soweþ   82
  þer-after he scal mowen;
and euerilces mannes dom   84
  to his ogen dure chariȝeþ.'

77. lagelice J; lagelich S.   80, 81. J *and* S *omit.*   82. þat te J;
that the S.   83. scal S; scall J.   84–86. J *omits.*   84. efr-
ilces S; *read* euerilces.   85. charigeth S (*for* chariȝeþ).

A. 5.

[þus queþ Alured:]
‘ þan knyhte bi-houeþ
   kenliche on to fóne   88
for to werie þat lond
   wiþ hunger and wiþ herivnge ;
þat þe chirche habbe gryþ,
   and þe cheorl beo in fryþ   92
his sedes to sowen,
   his medes to mowen ;
and his plouh beo i-dryue
   to vre alre bihoue :   96
þis is þes knyhtes lawe ;
   loke he þat hit wel fare !’

A. 6.

þvs queþ Alured :
‘ þe mon þe on his youhþe   100
   yeorne leorneþ
wit and wisdom,
   and iwriten reden,
he may beon on elde   104
   wenliche lorþeu.

86. A. *omits.*   91. A. *chireche.*

C. 5. þus cwaþ Alvred :
‘ þe cniht bihoueð
   ceneliche to cnowen   88
uor to werie þe lond
   of hunger and of heregong ;
þat te churche haue griþ,

87. bihoueð J ; behoveth S.   88. cnowen J ; mowen (!) S.
89. uor J ; nor (!) S.   werie J ; werce (!) S.   90. S *omits first* of.
91. þat te J ; that the S.   churche J ; Chureche S.

B. 5.

Þus qwad Alfred :
' Þe cniht bihouiþ
   kenliche to cnowen   88
forto weriin þe lond
   of here and of heregong ;
þat þe riche habbe gryþ,
   and the cherl be in friþ   92
his sedis to sowin,
   his medis to mowen ;
his plouis to driuin
   to ure alre bi-lif: 96
þis is þe cnihtes laȝe ;
   loke þat hit wel fare.'

[*This section is not found in* MS. B.]

87. cnith biouit.   88. cnouen.   91. *for* riche *read* chirche;
halbe (=habbe); gryt.   92. cherril ; frit.   93. souin.
97. cnich^s (*with* s *above the line*).

---

   and te cherl be in friþ   92
his sedes to sowen,
   his medes to mowen ;
his plowes to driuen
   to ure alre bilif: 96
þis is þe cnihtes lage,
   to locen þat it wel fare.'

92. te cherl J ; the cherle S.   95. his hise plowes J.   97. cnihtes S;
knihtes J.   98. wel J ; well S.   98. *Here* S *ends* ; J *omits* ll. 99-118.

And þe þat nule on youhþe
    yeorne leorny
wit and wisdom   108
    and iwriten rede,
þat him schal on elde
    sore rewe.
Þenne cumeþ elde   112
    and vnhelþe,
þenne beoþ his wéne
    ful wroþe isene.
Boþe heo beoþ bi-swike,   116
    and eke hi beoþ a-swunde.'

A. 7.

Þus queþ Alured:
' Wyþ-vte wysdome
    is weole wel vnwurþ;   120
for þey o mon ahte
    hundseuenti acres,
and he hi hadde isowen
    alle myd reade golde,   124
and þat gold greowe
    so gres doþ on eorþe,
nere he for his weole
    neuer þe furþer,   128
bute he him of [fremde]
    freond iwurche;
for hwat is gold bute ston,
    bute-if hit haueþ wis mon?'   132

106. A. one; *read* on ; *see* l. 104.   129. A. frumþe (*see note*).
130. A. iwrche.   132. A. wismon.

B. 6.

Þus qʊad Alfred :
‘ Wiðuten wisdom[e]
   is wele ful vnwurð;   120
for þau[h] o mon hadde
   ֝ hunt-seuiʊti acreis,
and he [is hauede sowen
   al] mid rede golde,   124
and þe gold grewe
   so gres deþ on þer erþe,
ne were his wele
   nouht þe vurþere,   128
bote he him [of] fremede
   frend y-ⱳerche.
For hⱳat is gold buᴛe ston,
   bute it habbe ⱳis mon?’   132

118. helfred.   119–132. *Preserved in* J.   119. wiðuten J
(*correctly*); wid ⱳidutin (!).   *Both* wisdom.   120. welðe wel
unwurð J; wele ful vnwrd.   121. þau; þoh J. man J. ahte J (*for* hadde);
B. *has* h . . de (h *at the edge, and letters cut away*; de *at beginning
of next line*).   122. aceres J.   123. *and* he as heȝed saȝin; *and*
hes hauede sowen J.   124. al J; *which* B. *omits*.   125. te J
(*for* þe).   gold grewe J; B. golde gre . . (*cut away*).   126. swo
gras doð on erðe J; so gres deit [*for* deith = deth] on þe rerþe (*second*
r *above the line*).   127. i . (*at the edge ; for* is = his); his J.   welðe J.
128. nout þe wrþere; ṅoht wurþ J.   129. hime J.   of *cut away ; but
supplied in* J.   fremðe J.   130. frende iwurche J.   131. uor J.
ⱳad; hwat J.   g . . . (*imperfect*); gold J.   but J.   132. id; it J.
halbe ₌ habbe; haue J.   man J.

A. 8.

Þus queþ Alured :

'Ne scolde neuer yong mon
 howyen to swiþe,

þeih him his wyse   136
 wel ne lykie ;

ne þeih he ne welde
 al þat he wolde.

For God may yeue, þenne he wule,   140
 god after vuele,

weole after wowe ;
 wel him þat ischapen is !'

A. 9.

Þus seyþ Alured :   144

'Strong hit is to rowe
 a-yeyn þe séé þat floweþ ;

so hit is to swynke
 . a-yeyn vnylimpe.   148

Þe mon þe on his youhþe
 [yeorne] swo swinkeþ,

and worldes weole her iwinþ,

   152

þat he may on elde
 idelnesse holde,

134. A. yongmon.
and hit. 145. A. reowe.
A line (or part of one) lost.
143. A. is him þat hit ischapen ; *I omit* is
150. *I supply* yeorne ; *cf.* l. 101. 152.

B. 7.

Þus quad Alfred :
'Shulde nefere *w*is mon
    ȝiuen hi*m* to uuele,
Þoch he his *w*ise   136
    *w*el ne like ;
ne Þeoh he ne welde :
    al Þat he *w*olde.
For God may ȝiuen, Þanne he *w*ele,   140
    good aft*er* yuil,
*w*ele after wrake ;
    so *w*el him Þet mot shapen.'

B. 8.

Þus quad Alfred :   144
'Stronge it is to ro*w*en
    aȝen Þe se-flod ;
so it is to s*w*inkin
    again unselÞe.   148
Ac *w*el is him a-ȝueÞe
    Þe [swich swinker] *w*as,
Þane*n* her on *w*erlde
    *w*elÞe to *w*inne*n*,   152
[Þat] he muȝe on elde
    ed[i]nesse holdin,

134. Sulde; ȝise (!)   135. huuele.   136. ȝise (*for* wise).   139. Þad.
140. *w*anne (*for* Þanne).   141. goed.   143. se (*read* so); scapen.
145. [. . . .]nge (*first four letters cut away*); his (*for* is); roȝen
(*for* ro*w*en).   147. [.]o; s *cut away*; his (*for* is); sȝinkin (*for*
s*w*inkin).   148. hunselÞe.   149. [.]ch (*for* Ach = Ac); *the* A *is
cut away*; aȝueÞe (*for* a-ȝueÞe, i. e. *in youth*).   150. Þe suinch *w*as
(*where* suinch *seems to be due to the confusion of* suinker *with* suich).
151. ẏane*n* (*for* Þane*n*); *altered to* ẏape*n* *by a later hand.*   153. Þat
cut away ; helde.   154. hednesse (*for* ed[i]nesse).

and ek myd his worldes weole
God iqueme er he quele;⠀⠀⠀⠀⠀⠀⠀⠀⠀156
youþe and al þat he haueþ idrowe
is þenne wel bi-towe.'

A. 10.

þus queþ Alured:
'Monymon weneþ⠀⠀⠀⠀⠀⠀⠀⠀⠀⠀⠀⠀160
⠀⠀þat he wene ne þarf,
longes lyues;
⠀⠀ac him lyeþ [þat] wrench!
For þanne [he] his lyues⠀⠀⠀⠀⠀⠀164
⠀⠀alre best luuede,
þenne he schal léten
⠀⠀lyf his owe.

For nys no wurt wexynde⠀⠀⠀⠀⠀168
⠀⠀a wude ne a velde,
þat euer mvwe þas feye
⠀⠀furþ vp-holde.

Not no mon þene tyme⠀⠀⠀⠀⠀⠀172
⠀⠀hwanne he schal heonne turne;
ne no mon þene ende
⠀⠀hwenne he schal heonne wende.

Dryhten hit one wot,⠀⠀⠀⠀⠀⠀⠀176
⠀⠀doweþes louerd,
hwanne [we] vre lif
⠀⠀leten schule.'

157. *Perhaps omit* al *or* þat.⠀⠀⠀163. A. þe wrench; *read* þat wrench, *as in* B.⠀⠀164. *I supply* he; *as in* B.⠀⠀168. A. wrt.⠀⠀A. uexynde; *read* wexynde, *as in* l. 433.⠀⠀178. *I supply* we; *as in* B.

[þat h]e mihte [mid] his welþe
    werchin Godis wille; 156
[þ]enne is his ӡueþe
    swiþe wel bitoӡen.'

B. 10. (*See* 9 *at* l. 180.)

þus quad Alfred:
'Monimon weniþ 160
    þat he wenen ne þarf,
longes liuis;
    ac him schal leӡen þat wrench!
For þanne he his lif 164
    alre beste trowe,
þenne shal he letin
    lif his oӡene.
Nis no wurt woxen 168
    on wode ne on felde,
þet euure muӡe
    þe lif up-helden.
wot no mon þe time 172
    hwanne he shal henne rimen;
ne no mon þen ende
    hwen he shal henne wenden.
Drihtin hit one wot, 176
    domis louird,
hwenne we ure lif
    letin schullen.'

---

155. [þat h] *cut away*; miſt = miht (*for* mihte); *I supply* mid.
157. enne (þ *cut away*) his his ӡeuþe. 160. wenit. 163. scal.
164. is (*for* his). 165. trowen (*against grammar*). 166. sal.
169. wdode (!); no (*for* ne). 173. wanne; sal. 174. hende.
175. wen (*initial* h *cut away*); sal. 176. Drittin. 178. wenne.
179. scullen.

A. 11.

þus queþ Alured: 180
'Yf þu seoluer and gold
    yefst and weldest in þis world,
neuer vpon eorþe
    to wlonk þu ny-wurþe.   184
Ayhte nys non ildre istreon,
    ac hit is Godes lone;
hwanne hit is his wille,
    þar-of we schulle wende,   188
and vre owe lyf
    myd alle for-leten.
þanne schulle vre ifon
    to vre veoh gripen,   192
welden vre madmes,
    and leten vs by-hinde.'

A. 12.

þus queþ Alured:
'Ne ilef þu nouht to fele   196
    uppe þe séé þat floweþ.
If þu hafst madmes
    monye and inowe,
gold and seoluer,   200
    hit schal gnyde to nouht;
to duste hit schal dryuen.
    Dryhten schal libben euere.

183. A. vpen (*for* vpon).   184. A. ny wrþe.   192. A. vouh (o
for e, *and* u *for* o).   193. A. Mayþenes (!); *see* l. 198.

B. 9. (*See* 10 *at* l. 159.)

þus quad Alfred :   180
'ȝif þu hauest welþe
    a wold in þis werlde,
ne þinc þu neure for-þi
    al to wlonc wurþen.   184
Ahte nis non eldere stren,
    ac it is Godis lone;
hwanne hit is his wille,
    þer-fro we shullen wenden,   188
and ure oȝene lif
    mid sorw letin.
Þanne schullen ure fon
    to ure fe gripen,   192
welden ure madmes,
    and lutil us bimenen.'

B. 11.

þus quad Alfred :
'Leue þu þe nouht to swiþe   190
    up þe se-flod ;
ȝif þu hauest madmes
    monie and moch[e],
gold and siluir,   200
    it shal wurþen to nouht ;
to duste it shal driuen.
    Drihtin shal liuin eure.

---

182. i wif ȝerlde (*for* in þis werlde).   183. nc (*in* þinc) *written
with* c *partly over the* n.   185. Acte.   187. wanne.   188. sullen.
191. scullen.   195. alfret.   196. nout ; sẏiþe (*for* swiþe).
198. hawest.   199. moch ; *read* moche (*plural*).   201. it follen
(*sic*) ; nout.   202. sullin (*for* shal).   203. driftin sal.

Monymon for his gold   204
    haueþ Godes vrre,
and for his seoluer
    hym-seolue for-yemeþ,
for-yeteþ and forleseþ.   208

Betere him by-come   209
    iboren þat he nere !'

A. 13. (PART II.)

þus queþ Alured :
'Lvsteþ ye, mi leode!   212
    ower is þe neode !
And ich eu wil lére

wit and wisdom,   216
    þat alle þing ouer-goþ.
Syker he may sitte
    þe hyne haueþ to i-vere.
For þeyh his eyhte him a-go,   220
    his wit ne agoþ hym neuer-mo.
For ne may he for-vare
    þe hyne haueþ to vere,
þe [h]wile his owe lyf   224
    ileste mote.'

A. 14.

þus queþ Alured :
'If þu hauest seorewe,
    ne seye þu hit þan arewe ;   228

---

208. *A line lost after this ? (But not counted).*
read mi, *as in* l. 27.   214. *A line lost after this.*
228. A. seye þu hit nouht þan ; *omit* nouht ; *see* B.

212: A. me ;
224. A. wile.

Moni mon for his gold   204
    hauið Godis erre,
and þuruh his siluer
    his saulle he forleseð. •   207

       .   .   .

Betere him were   209
    iborin þat he nere!'

B. 12. (PART II.)

Þus quad Alfred :
' Lustlike lust me,   212
    lef [and] dere,
and ich her ȝu wille leren,
    þenes mine,
wit and wisdom   216
    þe[t] alle welþe ouer-goð.
siker he may [sitte],
    and hwo [him] mid senden.
For þoch his welþe him at-go,   220
    his wit ne wen[t] him neuere fro.
Ne may he neuir for-farin
    hwo him to sere haueþ,
hwilis þat his lif   224
    lesten may.'

B. 13.

Þus quad Alfred :
' ȝif þu hauist sorwe,
    ne say þu hit þin areȝe ;   228

---

204. is.   205. hauid; erre *or* eue (*very indistinct*).   206. þuruch
is.   207. is (*for* his) ; forlesed.   208. Two *lines appear to be lost, but
have been counted as one.*   215. þenes, *or* wenes.   216. wisdome.
217. þe (*for* þet). *Apparently* oure god ; *read* ouer-goð.   218.
B *omits* sitte.   219. hem mide ; *but read* him mid ; *see note.*   220.
weleþe.   221. is wid (*for* his wit) ; wen ; newere (*for* neuere).
222. newir (*for* neuir).   224. is.

seye hit þine sadelbowe,
   and ryd þe singinde forþ.
Þenne wile wene,
   þet þine wise ne con,   232
þat þe þine wise
   wel [þe] lyke !
Serewe if þu hauest,
   and þe erewe hit wot,   236
by-fore, he þe meneþ,
   by-hynde, he þe teleþ.
Þu hit myht segge swych mon
   þat [hit] þe ful wel on ;   240
wyþ-vte echere ore
   he on þe muchele more.
By-hud hit on þire heorte,
   þat þe eft ne smeorte.   244
Ne let þu hyne wite
   al þat þin heorte by-wite.'

A. 15.

Þus queþ Alured:
'Ne schal-tu neuere þi wif   248
   by hire wlyte cheose,
for neuer nóne þinge
   þat heo to þe bryngeþ.
Ac leorne hire custe,   252
   heo cuþeþ hi wel sone.

234. *I supply* þe ; *see* B.   239. A. swyhc.   240. *I supply*
hit ; *see* B.

sey it þin sadilboƿe,
   and rid þe singende.
Þanne saiþ þe mon
   þat ti ƿise ne can,   232
þat þe þine ƿise
   ƿel þe likiþ.
Soreʒe ʒif þu hauist,
   and te areʒe hit seð,   236
bi-foren, he þe bimenið,
   bi-hindin, he þe scarneð.
þu hit miht seien sƿich mon
   þat it þe ful wel on;   240
sƿich mon þu maist seien þi sor,
   he ƿolde þat þu heuedest mor!
For-þi hit, in þin herte one,
   for-hele hit ƿið þin areʒe.   244
Let þu neuere þin areʒe ƿitin
   al þet þin herte þenkeþ.'

B. 16. (14, *at* l. 427; 15, *at* l. 458.)

Þus qu*a*d Alfred:
'Ne shal þu [neuer] þi ƿif   248
   bi hire ƿlite chesen;
ne [hire] for non ahte
   to þine bury bringen,
er þu hire costes   252
   [lerne, þe he] cuþe.

229. seit (*for* sey it).   231. sait.   233. þɛd.   234. likit.
236. te*n* (*for* te; *wrongly*); sed.   237. bimenid.   238. scarned.
239. miſt (*for* miht).   240. þad; fulwel.   242. þad.
243. Þiin; *erasure after* herte.   244. wid.   246. þenket.
248–251. *Preserved in* J.   248. sal þu þi; gin þu nefre þi J.
249. be J.   250. *I supply* hire. achte; ehte J.   251. þi buri J.
252. her (*for* er).   253. *The line is incomplete, consisting of the sole word* cuþe.

For mony mon for ayhte
   vuele i-auhteþ;
and ofte mon of fayre   256
   frakele icheoseþ.
Wo is him þat vuel wif
   bryngeþ to his cotlyf!
So him is alyue   260
   þat vuele ywyueþ.
For he schal vppon eorþe
   dreori i-wurþe.
Monymon singeþ   264
   þat wif hom bryngeþ;
wiste he hwat he brouhte,
   wepen he myhte.'

A. 16.

Þus queþ Alured: 268
'Ne wurþ þu neuer so wod,
   ne so wyn-drunke,
þat éuere segge þine wife
   alle þine wille.   272
For if [heo] iseye þe bi-vore
   þine i-vo alle,
and þu hi myd worde
   i-wreþþed heuedest,   276
ne schulde heo hit lete,
   for þing lyuyinde,
þat heo ne scholde þe forþ vp-breyde
   of þine baleu-syþes!   280
Wymmon is word-wod,
   and haueþ tunge to swift;

262. A. vppen.   273. A. if þu iseye (!); *for* þu *read* heo.
279. *Perhaps omit* forþ.   281. A. woþ (*for* woð=wod); *read*
wod.

For moni mon for ahte
    iuele ihasteð;
and ofte mon on faire   256
    fokel cheseð.
*w*o is him þat iuel *w*if
    bringið to his cot-lif!
So [him] is oliue   260
    þat iuele *w*iueð.
For he shal him often
    dreri maken.'   263

[*Four lines lost.*]

B. 17.

Þus q*u*ad Alfred: 268
'*w*urþu neuere s*w*o *w*od,
    ne so [wyn]-drunken,
þat euere sai[ȝe] þu þi *w*if
    al þat þi *w*ille be.   272
For if hue seȝe þe biforen
    þine fomen alle,
and þu hire mid *w*orde
    *w*raþed hauedest,   276
he ne shold it leten,
    for þinge liuiȝinde,
þat he ne sholde þe up-breidin
    of þine bale-siþes!   280
*w*im*m*on is *w*ord-*w*od,
    and hauiþ tu*n*ge to s*w*ift;

254. achte.   255. ihasted.   257. fokel (*sic*) chesed.   258, 259.
Preserved in J.   258. ifel J.   259. brinhit to is; bringed to his J.
260. *I supply* him; his (*for* is).   261. *w*iued.   262. sal.
270. *I supply* wyn-.   271. sai; *see* l. 480.   273. hif.   275. mit.
276. *w*raȝed.   277. sold.   278. þinke liuihinde.   279. solde.
282. hauit tu*n*ke to s*w*ift.

þeyh heo wel wolde,
 ne may heo hi nowiht welde.' 284

A. 17.

Þus queþ Alfred:
'Idelschipe and ouer-prute,
 þat lereþ yong wif vuele þewes;
and ofte þat [heo] wolde 288
 do þat heo ne scholde;
þene vnþev lihte
 leten heo myhte,
if heo ofte a swóte 292
 for-swunke were;
þeyh hit is vuel to buwe
 þat beo nule treowe.
For ofte museþ þe kat 296
 after hire moder.
Þe mon þat let wymmon
 his mayster iwurþe,
ne schal he neuer beon ihurd 300
 his wordes louerd;
ac heo hine schal steorne
 to-trayen and to-teóne;
and selde wurþ he blyþe and gled, 304
 þe mon þat is· his wiues qued.
   [*No break in* A.]

  288. *I supply* heo.

þauh he hire-selue *wel wolde,*
ne mai he it no*wiht welden.*'   284

B. 21. (18, *at* l. 477 ; 19, *at* l. 343; 20, *at* l. 305*.)

Þus qu*a*d Alfred :
'Idilschipe and orgul-prude,
    þat leriþ ȝung *wif* leþere þe*wes,*
and often to þenchen   288
    don þat he ne scholde;

.   .   .   .

.   .   .   .

ȝif he for-s*wun*ken swoti *were*   292
    s*wo* hie ne þohte;
ac þoh hit is iuel to be*wen*
    þat [trewe] ben ne wille.
For ofte museð þe catt   296
    after þe mod*er.*
[Hwoso] lat his .*wif*
    his maist*er wur*þen,
[ne] shal he neuer ben   300
    his *wordes louerd;*
ac he shal him rere
    dreiȝe, and moni tene
ȿelliche haue*n.* Selden   304
    shal he ben on sele.'

283. þauc.   284. no*wit.*   285. alu*erid.*   286. Idilscipe.
287. lerit.   289. scolde.   290, 291. *Not in* B.   292. for-s*wúken.*
þuere, *or* wuere (*read* were).   293. þochte.   294. þoch ; beuen,
altered to bewen.   295. ter (!) ; *read* trewe.   ville (*for* wille).
296. muæed.   298–301. *Preserved in* J.   298. *wose;* hwoso J.
is; his J.   299. master wurden J.   300. sal ; ne scal J.   nefre J.
301. is ; his J.   302. sal.   303. dreiȝe (*sic*) ; *read* treiȝe
or treȝe ?   304. ha*wen* (*for* hauen).   305. sal.

Mony appel is bryht wiþ-vte,
    and bitter wiþ-inne;
so is mony wymmon   308
    on hyre fader bure;
schene vnder schete,
    and þeyh heo is schendful.
So is mony gedelyng   312
    godlyche on horse,
and is þeyh lutel wurþ; . . .
wlonk bi þe glede
    and vuel at þare neode.'   316

A. 18.

þus queþ Alured:
'[N]Eure þu, bi þine lyue,
    þe word of þine wyue
to swiþe þu ne aréde. . . .   320
If heo beo i-wreþþed
    myd worde oþer myd dede,
wymmon wepeþ for mod
    oftere þan for eny god;   324
and ofte, lude *and* stille,
    for to vordrye hire wille;

---

314. *A line seems to be missing here.*   318. *The illuminator has forgotten to prefix the initial (coloured)* N. *Perhaps omit* þu; *it occurs in* l. 320.   320. *A line seems to be missing here.*

B. 20.

þus q*u*ad Alfred:	305*
' Moni appel is *wi*ð-uten grene,	306
briht on leme,	306*
and bitter *wi*ð-i*n*nen.	
So is moni *w*immo*n*	308
i*n* hire [fader] bure;	
schene under schete,	
and þoh hie is [schondes ful]	311
i*n* an stondes h*w*ile.	311*
S*w*o is moni gadeling	
godelike on horse,	313
*w*lanc on *w*eiȝe	315
and un*w*urþ on *w*ike.'	

B. 25. (**21**, *at* l. 285; **22**, *at* l. 496; **23**, *at* l. 360;
24, *at* l. 515.)

þus q*u*ad Alfred:	
[' Ared-tu] noht to s*w*iþe	
þe *w*ord of þine *w*iue;	
. . . . . .	320
For þanne hue beð i*w*raþed	
mid *w*ordes oþer mid dedes,	
*w*immo*n* *w*epeð for mod	
oft*er* þa*n*ne for eni god;	324
and ofte, lude and stille,	
for to *w*urchen hire *w*ille,	

305*. alu*r*ed.   306–311. *Preserved in* J.   306. mani J.   wid-
uten; uten J.   306*. brit; brihte J.   leme (*sic*); beme J.   307.
bittere; bitter J.   *wi*d-i*n*nen; wiðinnen J.   308. his; is J.   mani
wi*n*man J.   309. faire (!); fader J.   310. scene J.   scete J.
311. þocke; þoh J.   scondes ful J. (*which* Trin. *omits !*).   311*.
wile.   317. alu*r*ed.   318. Aretu (= Arettu = Ared-tu; *see* A. 320);
noth.   321. bed iwrarþed (*for* iwraþed; *first* r *above the line*).
323. *w*eped.

Heo wepeþ oþer-hwile,
   for to do þe gyle.
Salomon hit haueþ i-sed,
   þat wymmon can wel vuelne red.   328

.   .   .   .   .   .

.   .   .   .   .

þe hire red foleweþ,
   heo bryngeþ hine to seorewe.   332
For hit seyþ in þe l[e]oþ,
   " as scumes, forteoþ ";
hit is ifurn iseyd,
   þat " cold red is quene red ";   336
hu he is vnlede
   þat foleweþ hire rede.
Ich hit ne segge nouht for-þan
   þat god þing [n]ys god wymmon,   340
þe mon þe hi may icheose
   and icouere over oþre.'

A. 19.

þus queþ Alured:
' Monymon weneþ   344
   þat he weny ne þarf,
freond þat he habbe
   þar me him vayre bi-hat;
seyþ him vayre bi-vore,   348
   and frakele bi-hynde.
So me may þane loþe
   lengust lede.

333. *For* loþ *read* leoþ; *see note.*   340. *For* ys *read* nys; *see* l. 707.
A letter has been erased before ys *in the* MS.   342. *No break in* A
after this line.

Hue wepeð oþer-hwile
   hwen hue þe wille biwilen.   328
Salomon hit hauith isaid,
   hue can moni yuel reid.   330
Hue ne mai hit non oþir don,   330*
   for wel erliche hue hit bi-gan.   331*
þe mon þat hire red folewiþ,   331
   he bringeþ him to seruȝe.

.   .   .   .   .   .

For hit is said in lede,
   "Cold red is quene red."   336

.   .   .   .   .   .

I ne sa[i]ȝe it nocht bi-þan
   þat god þing [n]is god wimmon,   340
þe mon þat michte hire cnowen
   and chesen hire from oþere.'

B. 19.

Þus quad Alfred:
'Mani mon weniþ   344
   þat he wenin ne þarf,
frend þat he habbe
   þer mon him faire bihait;
seieþ him faire bi-foren,   348
   fokel at-hinden.
So mon mai welþe
   lengest helden.

327. weped : wile.   328. þen (*for* wen = hwen).   329. hid hawit isait.   331*. herliche.   331. þad; folewid.   335, 336. *Preserved in* J.   335. uor it seiþ in þe led J.   336. cwene J.   339. Hi (*for* I); sawe (w *for* ȝ); *read* saiȝe.   340. is (*read* nis); vimmon.   341. þad; cnofwen (!).   343. alured.   344. wenit.   346. þad.   348. Seiet.

Ne ilef þu neuer þane mon   352
   þat is of feole speche,
ne alle þe þinge
   þat þu iherest singe.
Mony mon haueþ swikelne muþ,   356
   milde, and monne for-cuþ;
Nele he þe cuþe
   hwenne he þe wule bi-kache.'

A. 20.

þus queþ Alured: 360
' Þvrh sawe mon is wis,
   and þurh iselþe mon is glev;
þurh lesinge mon is loþ,
   and þurh luþre wrenches vnwurþ;   364
and þurh hokede honde þat he bereþ
   him-seolue he for-vareþ.
From lesynge þu þe wune,
   and alle vnþewes þu þe bi-schune;   368
so myht þu on þeode
   leof beon in alle leode.
And luue þyne nexte,
   he is at þe neode gód.   372
At chepynge and at chyrche
   freond þu þe iwurche
wyþ pouere and wiþ riche,
   wiþ alle monne ilyche.   376
þanne myht þu sikerliche
   sely sytte,

362. A. his elþe (!) ; *for* hiselþe = iselþe.   364. A. wrenches.
And vnwurþ; (*but* And *is the last word on the leaf, and the back of
the leaf begins with* vnwurþ. And þurh, &c. *The scribe at first omitted*
vnwurþ, *and then, when inserting it, forgot to strike out the former* And).
365. þat he bereþ *is perhaps superfluous.*   368. *Perhaps omit* þe.
373. chyreche.

Gin þu neuere leuen   352
    alle monnis spechen,
ne alle þe þinge
    þat þu herest singen.
For moni mon hauiþ fikil mod,   356
    and he is monne cuð;
Ne shaltu neuere knowen
    hwanne he þe wole bikechen.'

B. 23. (**20,** *at* l. 305*; **21,** *at* l. 285; **22,** *at* l. 496.)

Þus quad Alfred: 360
' Þurh saȝe mon is wis,
    and þurh selþe mon is gleu;
þurh lesin[ge] mon is loð,
    and þurh luþere wrenches vnwurþ;   364
And hokede honden make þen mon
    his heuid to lesen.
Ler þu þe neuer
    ouer mukil to leȝen;   368

.   .   .   .   .   .
    .   .   .   .

ac loke þine nexte,
    he is atte nede god;   372
and frendschipe o werlde
    fairest to wurchen
wið pouere and wið riche,
    wið alle men iliche.   376
Þanne maist þu sikerliche
    seli sittin,

354. þinke.   355. sinken.   356. hauit.   358. saltu; knewen (!).   359. þanne *or* wanne; bitechen, *altered to* bikechen; *cf.* bi-kache *in* A.   361, 362. þurch.   363. þurch lesin; *rest cut off.* 364. þurúh.   366. is hewit.   368. leþen (*error for* leȝen). 372. ate.   373. frendchipe.   375. wid (*twice*).   376. wid.

and ek faren ouer [londe]·
   hwider so beoþ þi wille.'   ·   380

A. 21.

þus queþ Alured:
'Alle world-ayhte
   schulle bi-cumen to nouhte;
and vyches cunnes madmes   384
   to mixe schulen i-multen;
and vre owe lif
   lutel hwile ileste.
For þeyh o mon   388
   wolde al þe worlde,
and al þe wunne
   þe þar-inne wunyeþ,
ne myhte he þar-myde his lif   392
   none hwile holde.
Ac al he schal for-leten
   on a litel stunde;
and schal vre blisse   396
   to balewe us iwurþe,
bute-if we wurcheþ
   wyllen Cristes.
Nu biþenche we   400
   þanne vs selue   400*
vre lif to leden
   so Crist vs gynneþ lere;

---

379. lond le (!); *for* londe.'   381. *No break in A. after* l. 380.
400, 400*. *Only* one *line in former edition.*

and faren ouer londe
　　hƿar-so beþ þi ƿille.'　　　　　　　380

B. 29. (24–28; ll. 515, 317, 410, 533, 556.)

þus qwad Aluℛed:
' Werldes ƿelþe
　　to ƿurmes shal ƿurþien;
and alle cunnes madmes　　　　　　384
　　to noht shulen melten:
and ure lif shal
　　lutel lasten.
For [þoh] þu, moℛ, ƿeldest　　　　388
　　al þis middelerd,
and alle þe ƿelþe
　　þat þer-inne ƿoniþ,
ne miht þu þi lif　　　　　　　　392
　　lengen none hƿile.
Bote al þu it shalt leten
　　one lutele stunde;
and al þi blisse　　　　　　　　396
　　to bale shal iƿurþen,
bote-ȝif þu ƿurche
　　ƿille to Cℛiste.
Foℛ[þi] biþenk[e] ƿe　　　　　　400
　　[on] þe wis us seluen　　　　　400*
to leden ure lif
　　so God us ginniᵹ̌ leℛen;

380. bet.　　　381. aluℛed.　　　383. scal.　　　385. nocht sulen.
386. ƿure (*read* ure *as in* l. 401); sal.　　388. *I supply* þoh.　　389.
middellert.　　　391. þad þe inne ƿonit.　　　392. miſt (*for* miht).
393. ƿile.　　　394. salt.　　　397. sal.　　　398. þif (*error for* ȝif).
400. for (*but read* Forþi); biþeng.　　400*. *I supply* on; þe uuiſ = þe
wis (*not* we mus l); selƿen.　　　402. ginnid leℛeℛ (*not* leteℛ).

þanne mawe we wenen
 þat he wule vs wurþie.   404
For so seyde Salomon,
 [Salomon] þe wise,   405*
þe mon þat her wel deþ,
 he cumeþ þar he lyen foþ;
on his lyues ende   408
 he hit schal a-vynde.'

A. 22.

þus queþ Alured:
' Ne gabbe þu ne schotte,
 ne chid þu wyþ none sotte; 412
ne myd manyes cunnes taleſ
 ne chid þu wiþ nenne dwales.
Ne neuer þu bi-gynne
 to telle þine tyþinges 416
'at nones fremannes borde ;
 ne haue þu to vale worde.
Mid fewe worde wis mon
 fele biluken wel con; 420
and sottes bolt is sone i-schote ;
 for-þi ich holde hine for dote
þat sayþ al his wille
 þanne he scholde beon stille. 424
For ofte tunge brekeþ bon,
 þeyh heo seolf nabbe non.'

404. A. wrþie. 405*. A *omits* Salomon. 409. *No break in* A.
after this line. 415. A. þu ne bi-gynne ; *omit* ne ; *see* B. 419.
A. wismon. 421. A. i-scohte. 426. *No break in* A. *after this line.*

þenne muȝe *w*e *w*enen
    þat he us *w*ile *w*urþen.   404

For swo saide Salomon,
    þe *w*ise Sal*om*on,   405*

*w*is is þat wel [deþ]
    h*w*ile he i*n* þis *w*erld[e] [beþ];

euere at þen ende   408
    he comið þer he hit findiþ.'

B. 26.

Þus q*ua*d Alfred :
'Be þu neuere to bold
    to chiden aȝen oni scold,   412

ne mid manie tales
    to chiden aȝen alle d*w*ales.

Ne neuere þu biginne
    to tellen ne*w*e tidinges   416

at neuere nones mo*n*nis bord;
    ne haue þu to fele *w*ord.

Þe *w*ise mon mid fe*w*e *w*ord
    can fele biluken;   420

and sottis bolt is sone ischote*n*;
    for-þi ich telle him for a dote

þat saiþ al his y-*w*ille
    þanne he shulde ben stille.   424

For ofte tunge brekiþ bo*n*,
    [þeih he habbe] hire-selue non.'

404. þad.   406. *w*is is þad *w*el doþ (*wrongly altered to* is þad *w*el doþ *w*is); *but read* deþ (*as in* A.), *for the metre.*   407. h*w*ile he is i*n* þis *w*erld boþ (*altered to* h*w*ile he i*n* þis *w*erld is boþ; is *being above the line*); *but* boþ *is an error for* beþ, *and* is *is needless.*   408. þe nende.   409. comid; findit.   418. ha*w*e.   421. bold; iscote*n*. 423. þad sait; is; *for* y-*w*ille *perhaps read* *w*ille; *see* l. 440. 424. sulde.   425, 426. *Preserved in* J.   425. tunke brekit; tunge breceþ J.   426. and nauid; þeih he habbe J (*much better*). hire sel*w*e; him selue J.

A. 23.

þus queþ Alured:
'Wis child is fader blisse.—   428
If hit so bi-tydeþ
    þat þu bern ibidest,
þe hwile hit is lutel
    ler him mon-þewes.   432
Þanne hit is wexynde,
    hit schal wende þar-to;
þe betere hit schal iwurþe
    euer buuen eorþe.   436
Ac if þu him lest welde,
    wexende on worlde,
lude and stille,
    his owene wille,   440
hwanne cumeþ ealde,
    ne myht þu hyne awelde;
þanne deþ hit sone
    þat þe biþ vnyqueme,   444
ofer-howeþ þin ibod,
    and makeþ þe ofte sory-mod.
Betere þe were
    iboren þat he nere;   448
for betere is child vnbore
    þane vnbuhsum.
Þe mon þe spareþ yeorde
    and yonge childe,   452
and let hit arixlye
    þat he hit areche ne may,
þat him schal on ealde
    sore reowe.' Amen.   456

438. A. werende; *see* l. 433.

Expliciunt dicta Regis Aluredi.

[*End of Text* A.]

B. 14.

Þus quad Alfred :

‘ Wis child is fadiris blisse.—　　　　　　　　　428

Ȝif it so bitidiþ

   þat þu child weldest,

þe hwile þat hit is litil

   þu lere him monnis þewis.　　　　　　　432

Þanne hit is woxin,

   he shal wende þerto ;

þanne shal [þi] child

   þas þe bet wurþen.　　　　　　　　　436

Ac ȝif þu les him welden

   .　　.　　.　　.　　.

.　　.　　.　　.　　.　　.

   al his owene wille,　　　　　　　　　440

þanne he comiþ to elde,

   sore it shal him rewen ;

and he shal banne þat wiht

   þat him first taȝte ;　　　　　　　　444

þanne shal þi child

   þi forbod ouer-gangin.

Beter þe were,

   child þat þu ne hauedest ;　　　　　　448

for betere is child vnboren

   þenne vnbeten.’

[*Six lines missing.*]

429. bitidit.　　430. þad; chil (*see* l. 428).　　431. wile.　　433. *Read* y-woxin ?　　434. sal wenne.　　435. sal. þe (*read* þi ; *see* l. 445).　　441. comit; helde.　　442. sal.　　443. sal; widt (!).　　445. sal.

B. 15.

þus quad Alfred :
'Drunken and vndrunkin,
 eyþer is *w*isdom *w*el god ;   460
þarf no mon drinkin þe lasse
 þan he be *w*ið-alle *w*is.
Ac [ʒif] he drinkiþ
 and desieþ þere amorʒe,   464
so þat he, fordrunken,
 desiende *w*ercheþ,
he shal ligen long a-nicht,
 litil shal he sclepen ;   468
him sukeþ soreʒe to
 so deð þe salt on fles[she] ;
sukeþ þuru his liche
 so [deþ þuru] liche blod.   472
and his morʒe-sclep
 shal ben muchil lestin[de],
[h*w*oso] þe s*w*o on euen
 yuele haueð ydronken.'   476

B. 18. (16, *at* l. 247 ; 17, *at* l. 268.)

þus quad Alfred :
'*w*urþu neuere so *w*od,
 ne so desi of þi mod,
 þat euere s[a]iʒe þi frend   480

460. eþer ; *w*isdome.   462. wid ale.   463. *I supply* ʒif (Kemble *supplies* ef) ; drinkit.   464. desiet.   466. werchet. 467. sal.   468. sal.   469. suʒh ; *read* sukeþ, *as in* l. 471. 470. salit ; fles (*for* flesh ; *but read* flesshe).   471. suket ; is. 472. dot (*for* deþ ; *see* l. 470). *I supply* þuru.   474. sal ; lestind ; d *erased*.   475. *w*erse (*corruptly*) ; *read* hwoso.   476. haued. 477. alu*e*rid.   480. þad.   siʒe ; *see* A. 271.

al þat þe likiþ,
ne alle þe þonkes
 þat þu þoh hauist;
for ofte sibbie men   484
 foken hem bituenen,
and ef it so bilimpiþ
 lo[þ]e þat ȝe wurþen,
þanne wot þi fend   488
 þat er wiste þi frend.
Betere þe bicome
 þi word were helden;
for þanne muð mameliþ   492
 more þanne hit sholde,
þanne schulen his eren
 ef[t] it iheren.'

  B. 22. (**19,** *at* l. 343; **20,** *at* l. 305*; **21,** *at* l. 285.)

Þus quad Alfred: 496
'ȝif þu frend bi-ȝete
 mid þi fre biȝete,
loke þat þu him þeine
 mid alle þeuues þine,   500
loke þat he þe be mid
 bi-foren and bi-hinden;
þe bett he shal þe reden
 at alle þine neden;   504
on him þu maist þe tresten
 ȝif his trowþe deȝh.

481. likit. 483. þoch. 486. bilimpit. 487. lo . e (*letter erased between* o *and* e). 489. þad her viste. 492. mud mamelit. 493. solde. 494. sculen; heren. 495. ef. 496. alfreuerd (!). 500. þines; *see note.* 501. mide. 503. sal. 505. and on (and *is not wanted*). 506. þif (*error for* ȝif); is troȳþe (ȳ *for* w).

Ac ȝif þu hauist a frend to-day,
  and to-moreuin driuist him awei,   508
þenne bes þu one
  al-so þu er were;
and þanne is þi fe for-loren,
  and þi frend boþen;   512
betere þe bicome
  frend þat þu neuedest.'

B. 24. (23, *at* l. 360.)

Þus quad Alfred:
'ȝif þu hauist duȝeðe,   516
  and drihten [it] þe sendeþ,
ne þenk þu neuere þi lif
  to narruliche leden,
ne þine faires   520
  to faste holden.
For þer ahte is [i]hid,
  þer is armþe i-noh;
and siker ich it te saȝe,
  letet ȝif þe likeþ,   525
swich mon mai after þe
  þi god welden,   } 526
ofte binnen þine burie   527
  bliþe wenden,

510. her.   511. *Perhaps omit* and.   514. newedest.   515. aluerd
or alured.   516-532. *Preserved in* J.   516. duȝe; duȝeðe J.
517. drichen; drihten J.   it *supplied from* J.   te (*for* þe) J.   senden (!);
sendeþ J.   518. þeng; gin J.   519. narwlice J.   520. *Both*
faires.   521. helden J.   522. hachte; ehte J.   hid; ihud J.
523. soreȝe (*for* armþe) J.   inoch; inoh J.   524. J *omits* and.   ic J.
seȝȝe J.   525. lef it if J.   liket; liceð J.   526. *Two lines
miscounted as one.*   swulc man J.   welðe (*for* god) J (*better*).   527.
binne þi buri J.   528. sitten (*for* wenden) J.

þat [þe] ne *w*ele heren
  mid muþe mone3en;
ac euere him of-þinkeþ
  þen he [of] þe þenkeð.' 532

B. 27. (25, *at* l. 317; 26, *at* l. 410.)

Þus q*u*ad Alu*r*ed:
'Elde cumið to tune
  mid fele vnkeþe costes,
and doþ þe mon to elde*n*, 536
  þat ne mai he him noht *w*elden.
Hit makiþ him *w*el vn-meke,
  and binimiþ him his mi3te.
3if it s*w*o bitideð 540
  þat þu her so longe abidist,
and þu in þin elde
  *w*erldes *w*elþe *w*eldest,
þi du3eþe gin þu delen 544
  þine dere frend[e]
h*w*ile þine da3es du3en,
  and þu þe-seluen liue mo*w*e.
Haue þu none leue to [þo] 548
  þat after þe bileueð,
to sone ne to douhter,
  ne to none of þine foster.
For fe*w*e frend *w*e schulen finden 552
  þanne *w*e henne funden;

529. þad. he; te (*for* þe) J; *read* þe.   wile J.   530. muni3en J.
531. euuere; efre J.   of þinket; of þincheþ J.   532. hwanne (*for*
þen) J.   *I supply* of *from* J.   þenked; þencheþ J.   534. cumid.
536. helde*n*.   537. þat him sel*w*e ne mai he him noch *w*elden; *but*
him *means* 'himself,' *and* him sel*w*e *is superfluous*.   538. makit.
539. binimit; is mifte.   540. bitided.   542. þiin helde.   545. frend.
547. sel*w*en.   548. þe; *read* þo.   549. þad; bileued.   550. douter.
552. sculen.

for he þat is ute bi-loken
  he is inne sone for-ȝeten.'

B. 28.

þus quad Alured: 556
' ȝif þu i þin elde
  best welþes bidelid,
and þu ne cunne þe leden
  mid none cunnes listis,   560
ne þu ne moȝe mid strenȝþe
  þe-seluen steren,
þanne þanke þi louerd
  of alle his lone,   564
and of alle þine owene liue,
  and of þe daȝis liht[e],
and of alle murþe
  þat he for mon makede;   568
and hweder-so þu wendes,
  sei þu, atten ende,
" wurþe þat iwurþe,
  iwurþe Godes wille ! " '   572

B. 30. Part III. (29, *at* l. 381.)

þus quad Alured:
' Sone min swo leue,
  site me nu bisides,
and ich þe wile seiȝen   576
  soþe þewes.—
Sone min, ich fele
  þat min her falewiþ,

557. helde.   561. strenȝhe.   562. selwen.   564. is; loue
or lone.   566. litht.   568. þad.   569. hwendes. 570. aten-
ende.   571. wrþe þad.   576. hich; sigen.   579. þad;
falewidþ.

and min wlite is wan,   580
   and min herte woc.
Mine daʒis aren nei done,
   and we shulen unc to-delen;
wenden ich me shal   584
   to þis oþir werlde,
and þu shalt bileuen
   in alle mine welþe.
Sone min, ich þe bidde,   588
   þu art mi barin dere,
þat þu þi folk[e] be
   fader, and for louerd;
fader be þu wið child,   592
   and be þu widewis frend;
þe arme gin þu froueren,
   and þe woke gin þu coueren;
þe wronge gin þu rihten   596
   mid alle þine mihten;
and let þe, sune, mid lawe,
   and louien þe [shal] driʒten;
and ouer alle oþir þinge   600
   God be þe ful [in] minde,
and bide þat he þe rede
   at alle þine dedis;
þe bet shal [he] þe filsten   604
   to don al þine wille.'

---

582. arren.   583. sulen.   584. sal.   586. salt.   589. ard;
barin (= barn, i. e. bairn).   590. þad; folck (*read* folke).   592. wid.
593. wuidewis (wui = uui = wi).   594. ginne; *read* gin.   595, 596.
ginne; *read* gin.   596. wronke; riften.   597. miften.   599. lowien
(w = u); sulen (*but read* shal, *which I write in place of it*).   600. ower
(w = u); þinke.   601. *I supply* in.   602. þad.   604. sal; *I*
supply he.

B. 31.

þus qu*ad* Alur*e*d:
‘Sone mi*n* so dere,
  do so ich þe lere.   608
Be þu *w*is on þi *w*ord[e]
  and *w*ar o þine speche;
þenne shulen þe louien
  leden alle.   612
Þe ȝunge mon do þu la*w*e,
  [þan] elde lat' his lond hauen.
Drunken mon ȝif þu metes
  i*n* weis oþer i*n* stretes,   616
þu ȝef him þe *w*eie reme,
  and let him forð gliden.
Þanne miht þu þi lond
  mid frendschipe helden.   620
Sone, þu best bus [to]
  þe sot of bismare-*w*ord,
and bet him siþen þer-mide
  þat him ginne to smerten.   624
And, baren, ich þe bidde,
  ȝif þu on benche sittest,
and þu þen beuir hore sixst
  þe bi-foren sto*n*de*n*,   628
buh þe from þi sete,
  and bide him sone þer-to;
þanne *w*elle he saȝi*n*
  sone on his *w*orde,   632

609. *w*ord; *see* l. 632.   611. sulen; lo*w*ien.   614. þad (*sic*),
for þat; *read* þan, *masc. acc.*; helde; is; ha*w*en.   615. ȝif (*altered
to* þif; *read* ȝif); mestes (!).   618. ford.   619. miſt.   620. mit
frendchipe.   621. best bus (*sic*); *I supply* to.   624. þad.   625.
baren = barn (i. e. bairn).   626. þif; sitthest.   629. buch.   631.
ſa*w*i*n* (*for* saȝi*n*).   632. one; *see* l. 609.

"wel worþe þe [wite]
 þat þe first taȝte!"
Site þanne siþin
 bisiden him-seluen,   636
for of him þu miȝt leren
 listis and fele þeues;
þe baldure þu miȝt ben;
 lere þu his reides!   640
for þe elder mon me mai of-riden
 betere þenne of-reden.'

B. 32.

þus quad Alured:
'Sone min so dere,   644
 ches þu neuere to fere
þen luþere lusninde mon;
 for he þe wile wrake don.
From þe wode þu miht te faren   648
 wið wilis and wið armes;
ac þanne þu hit lest wenest,
 þe luþere þe biswikeþ.
þe bicche bitiþ ille   652
 þauh he berke stille;
so deþ þe lusninde luþere mon,
 ofte, hwen he dar it don;
hwan he be wiþ-uten stille,   656
 he bit wiþ-innin ille.

633. wid (!).   634. þad; taite; *read* taȝte.   635. fete (*read*
Site); seiþen.   637. miſt.   639. *Read* balder; miſt.   640. for
lere; *I omit* for, *as it is needless; perhaps it was copied from* l. 641.
641. helder.   648. fron (!); mitht; te (*for* þe, *after* t).   649. wid
(*twice*).   650. hid.   651. biswiket.   652, 653. *Preserved in* J.
652. biche J.   bitit; biteþ J.   653. þau; þoh J.   berce J.   654.
deit; *read* deth = deþ.   655. wen; darit.   656. wan.   657. hille.

and al bi-fuliþ he his frend
hwen he him vnfoldiþ.'

B. 33.

þus quad Alured :   660
' Leue sone dere,
   ne ches þu neuere to fere
þen hokerfule lese mon ;
   for he þe wole gile don.   664
He wole stelin þin ahte and keren,
   and listeliche onsuerren ;
so longe he wole be [þe] bi,
   he wole bringin on and tuenti   668
to nouht, for soþe ich tellit þe ;
   and oþer he wole liȝen
   and hokerful ben þuru hoker,   } 670
and lesing þe aloþeð
   alle men þat hen ycnoweð.   672
Ac nim to þe a stable mon
   þat word and dede bi-sette con,
and multeplien eure god ;
   a such fere þe is help in mode.'   676

B. 34.

þus quad Alured :
' Leue sone dere,
   ne ches þu neuere to fere

658. he bi-fulit; *read* bi-fuliþ he.   659. wen ; vnfoldit.   661. lewe (w = u).   665. haite (*for* ahte).   667. uole; *I supply* þe.   668. uole brinhin.   669. nout ; tellit = telle it.   670. liþen (*for* liȝen) ; *this passage is corrupt.*   671. aloþed.   672. ycnowed.   673. nim þe to þe ; *I omit the former* þe.   675. heure; *for* eure *or* ȝure.   676. sug (!), *with* g = j (suj *for* such) ; his (*for* is) ; mode (*sic* ; *hardly for* niod = neod, *i. e.* need).   679. neuerre.

littele mon, ne long, ne red,   680
   ʒif þu wult don after mi red.

B. 35.

Þe luttele mon he is so rei,
   ne mai non him wonin nei;
so worð he wole him-seluen ten,   684
   þat his louird maister he wolde ben;
bute he mote himseluen pruden,
   he wole maken fule luden;
he wole grennen, cocken, and chiden,   688
   and euere faren mid vn-luden.
ʒif þu me wult ileuen,
   ne mai me neuer him quemen.

B. 36.

Þe longe mon is leþe-bei,   692
   selde comið his herte rei;
he hauiþ stoni herte,
   no-þing him ne smerteþ;
bi forð daʒes he is aferd   696
   of sticke and ston in huge werd;
ʒif he falliþ in þe fen,
   he þewiþ ut after men;
ʒif he slit in-to a diche,   700
   he is ded witerliche.

681. þif; wld (*for* wuld = wult).   682. his.   684. word.
685. is.   689. hewere (*w for* u).   690. þif; wld.   692. lonke
(*see* l. 680).   693. comid is.   694. hauit.   696. ford.
698. þif; fallit.   699. þewit.   700. þif; adige (*read* a diche).

B. 37.

þe rede mon he is a qued,
    for he *w*ole þe þin iuil red;
he is cocker, þef, and horeling,   704
    scolde, of *w*reche-dome he is king.
Ich ne s[e]iȝe nouht bi-þan
    þat moni ne be*n* gentile man;
þuru *w*is lore and genteleri[e]   708
    he amendiþ huge companie.

702. aquet (*read* a qued).   703. i*w*il (*for* iuil) ; red (*sic*).   706.
Hic (*for* Ich) ; sige (*read* seiȝe) ; nout.   709. amendit.

NOTES

Throughout ll. 1–456 the words cited are from Text A, unless B or C is expressly prefixed.

LINE 1. *Seuorde* (B *Siforde*; C *Sifforde*); Seaford, near Newhaven, on the south coast of Sussex. Formerly a Roman station, and a port of some importance at the mouth of the Ouse, until the great storm of 1570 altered the river's course, and caused the rise of Newhaven, which took its place and owes its name to this circumstance (Imperial Cyclopaedia). The casual guess that the reference is to Shefford (Berks. or Beds.) is valueless, as the Sheffords are remote from the use of the southern dialect.

4. See l. 66. Apparently imitated from Layamon, who has similar lists of counsellors. Thus, at l. 14620, we find mention of 'earls, warriors, bishops and "boc-ilæred" men, and thanes'. At l. 16912, the king greets his 'earls, warriors, bishops, and "boc-ilærede" men'. And at l. 21857, we find 'three wise bishops, very learned in books (*a boke wel ilæred*), priests and monks, very many'.

6. *egleche*, bold, valiant; an uncommon word. It occurs again in 'Sleiʒe men and *egleche*'; Sammlung altenglischer Legenden, ed. Horstmann, 1878; *Magdalena*, l. 1 (p. 148). And again, *egleche* is an epithet of the Empress Matilda in Robert of Gloucester, ed. W. A. Wright, Appendix XX. 125 (p. 847). A.S. *āglēca*, a cruel person, fierce warrior, common in poetry, and allied to *āglāc*, calamity, fierce fight, a word of uncertain origin. See Grein and Bosworth. For words not explained in these Notes, see the Glossary.

7. *Alurich*; A.S. *Ælfrīc*, the commonest of A.S. names.

8. *þare*, A.S. *þǣre*; fem. dat. For remarks on the grammatical forms, see the Preface.

9. *Ealured*, Ælfred (now Alfred) the Great, here called *Englene hurde*, shepherd of the Angles (English), and *Englene durlyng*, darling of the Angles. So also in Layamon, l. 6316, we find 'Alfred the king' described as 'Engelondes deorling'. It is remarkable that Layamon likewise describes 'king Vortimer' as being 'Bruttene deorling' (l. 14937); 'Arthur the king' as being 'Bruttene deorling' (ll. 21928, 25118); and 'Angel the king' as being 'Scottene deorling' (l. 25576), and 'Scotlondes deorling' (l. 25184); and see ll. 23828, 23834.

12 (and 17). The form *Englene-lond* is, of course, wrong (see B and C), and was caught up from ll. 10, 11; it encumbers the line. The usual A.S. name for England was *Engla-land*, where *Engla* is the gen.

of *Engle* (also *Angle*, as in the A.S. translation of Beda), nom. pl. 'the Angles'. *Englene* was a later (M.E.) form, due to the not unfrequent substitution of *-ene* (A.S. *-ena*, weak form) for *-e* (A.S. *-a*, strong form), in genitives plural. Thus we find *king-ene*, of kings, *clerk-en* (shortened from *clerk-ene*), of clerks, in Piers Plowman, B. i. 105, iv. 119.

13. For *bi-gon* read *gon* (B *gon*; C *gan*); it scans better :—'Héom he gòn lére.' *Gon* is used, like our *did*, as a mere auxiliary :—' Them did he teach, as ye may hear, how they should lead their life.'

14. B *we*. Here, as in many other places, there is a confusion of symbols (see the Preface). The *w* (A.S. ꝥ in the MS.) is an error for ȝ, so that the sense is 'ye'. In l. 15 we might make the same correction, giving the sense—'how ye should lead your life'; but it is obvious (see A and C) that the scribe has mistaken the sense altogether, and that the right reading is *hu hi hure lif*, with *hure* for *hire*, 'their.' The amended spellings in B can usually be understood by comparison with A and with the usual spellings of the thirteenth century.

17. It is clear that the reading in B is later than that of A; *and lufsum thing* has been added, to make a rime; whilst at the same time *a king* has been transferred to l. 17. But this makes l. 17 too long; the writer should also have deleted the word *Alfred*, and he would then have had a perfect couplet.

21. *word* should rather be *worde*, in the dat. case, as in l. 632. Cf. also ll. 609, 610.

24. B *in E. on*; C *on E. on*. 'The use of the two prepositions before and after the sb. is very curious, but pretty frequent in Early English writers'; E. Gropp, note on the line. I do not think it is at all 'frequent', and it will be noted that no example is cited! Koch (Gramm. ii. 354) cites from the A.S. Chron. an. 894—'ær hie wæron *inne on* þam geweorce,' ere they were within inside that fort; also *an inne* (on within) from Layamon, l. 5617, 15426. But surely *in* should be deleted; it is not in A. Or *on* should be omitted, as in two of the three transcripts of C.

30. *wisliche*, verily, of a surety; adv. So also *wislike* in Havelok, l. 274, where I explain it by 'wisely' (which is a possible sense). 'Would ye, my people, listen to your lord, he would verily teach you things, how ye might enjoy the world's honours, and also unite your souls to Christ.' In B, the words *and* (l. 29) and *of* (l. 30) are both superfluous.

37, 38. The sense in A and C is clear; but B has lost a part of the sentence, and probably *dom* is an error for *dome*, dative. Then the sense would be—'[Mildly I advise you, my dear friends], both poor people and rich, concerning the doom of life.' For *edi* (in C) read *edie*, pl., answering to A.S. *ēadige*, pl. of *ēadig*, prosperous, rich.

45. *one*, alone, A.S. *āna*. 'He alone is good, above all goodness.'

47. 'He alone is wise, above all gladness.' Here *glednesse* looks like an error for *gleawnesse*, wisdom; but note the remarkable reading 'glad things' in B.

51. *monne*, A.S. *manna*, gen. pl., of men. The reading *mon* (in B) is absurd. 'He alone is the mildest master of men.'

57. *wone*, A.S. *wana*, esp. used in the phrase *wana wesan*, to be wanting (Toller). 'That no part of his desire shall be lacking to him (i. e. the man), who here in this world intends to worship Him.'

67. The reading *wyttes* (A) is an obvious error for *writes* (B C). 'Unless he be learned in books, and be very well acquainted with his writings (manuscripts), and know how to observe letters entirely by himself, (so as to know) how he ought lawfully to govern his land.' C has *icweme*, 'please,' which requires the reading *him*. Layamon has the sb. *writ*, 'a letter,' the pl. being both *writen* and *writes*. See ll. 103, 109 below.

80, 81. Not in B C. See the correction in the footnote. The sense is—'The poor and the rich they shall judge alike,' i. e. impartially.

82. 'Quae enim seminauerit homo, haec et metet'; Galat. vi. 8 (7). Compare The Owl and the Nightingale, ll. 1037–40. For remarks on the various Proverbs, see p. 71.

83. The strange form *alsuipich* in B evidently means 'alsuiwich'— with *p* for *w*—an error for *al suich* (confused with *al swich*).

84. 'And every man's judgement will return to his own door.'

87. 'It behoves the knight valiantly to undertake to defend the land against famine and invasion.' B C have *cnowen*, i. e. to know how to. The phrase *fon on*, to take on, undertake, occurs again in Layamon, iii. 263, l. 31415. It answers to the A.S. *on-fōn*.

96. 'To the profit of us all.' B has 'for the sustenance of us all'; but *bilif* should certainly be *bilive*, as the A.S. form is *bīleofa*; see *Bylive* in N. E. D.

103. *iwriten*, writings, pl. of *iwrit*. The same as *writes*, pl. of *writ*, in l. 67. Cf. l. 109.

105. *wenliche*, pleasant, acceptable; A.S. *wĕnlīc*, fair, comely; not common. We find *wenlukest*, most lovely, in Old Eng. Homilies, ii. 29, l. 12; *wenliche*, very fair, translating Lat. *speciosa*, id. ii. 83, l. 9.

lorþeu, teacher. The old A.S. word was *lārēow*. It occurs in John, i. 38, in all the MSS. except the latest (Hatton MS.), which substitutes for it the form *lārðēow*, formed like *lādtēow* (for *lād-ðēow*) with the word *ðēow* (servant) as a suffix. After all it is highly probable that *lārēow* is a worn down pronunciation of *lārðēow* itself. See *Larew* in N. E. D.

114. 'Then his expectations will be apparent (as being) very

perverse'; i.e. will seem to be very disappointing. *Isene* answers, rightly, to the A.S. adj. *gesȳne*, visible, evident, rather than to the pp. of the verb *to see*; so that *wroþe* is the A.S. *wrāþe*, adj. pl.

116. 'They both (i.e. wit and wisdom) will be disappointed, and moreover they will be wasted away.'

119. In *wid widutin* (B, *as in* Trin. MS.) the syllable *wid* is absurdly repeated; see A :—'Without wisdom is wealth very worthless.'

122. *hundseuenti*, 70. The Old English numeration shows traces of the use of the 'great hundred', i.e. 120. Thus we find *twentig*, 20; *þritig*, 30; *feowertig*, 40; *fiftig*, 50; *siextig*, 60; at which point the first half of the great hundred was completed. Higher numbers take the prefix *hund-*, giving the series *hundseofontig*, 70; *hundeahtatig*, 80; *hundnigontig*, 90; *hundteontig* (or *hund*), 100; *hundendlufontig*, 110; *hundtwelftig*, 120. So that both *eleventy* and *twelfty* were once in use.

123. A 'and he had sown them'; where *hi* denotes 'them'. The Trinity MS. of B has—'*and* he as heȝed saȝin'; while the James MS. has—'*and* hes hauede sowen.' It is clear that 'heȝed' is miswritten for 'heued', a by-form of 'hauede', i.e. had. Also, that 'saȝin' is miswritten for 'sawin', i.e. sown. The text is best mended by adopting *hauede sowen* from the James MS. A difficulty remains, viz. what are we to understand by the readings *he as* (T) and *hes* (J)? Certainly, *he as* should be corrected to *he is*, meaning 'he them', as in A. The reading *hes* is for *he's*, the same thing, but with elision. Dr. Morris, in his Preface to Genesis and Exodus, p. xviii, fully illustrates the use, chiefly in the southern dialect, of *is* = 'them'; and especially notices the use of *hes* = *he* + *is*, as in Gen. and Ex., ll. 911, 943. Again, in the Bestiary, l. 12, we have—'ðat he ne cunne *is* finden,' i.e. that he may not be able to find *them*; and in l. 173—'If ðu hauest *is* broken,' i.e. if thou hast broken *them*.

126. *so*, as. The reading in B (Trin. MS.) is rather indistinct, but is really *so gres deit on þe rerþe*, where the last *r* is above the line and is small, so that both Kemble and Wright read it as *reiþe*. All that is wrong is that *deit* is for *deþ* (doth), and *þe rerþe* is for *þer erþe* (the earth), the form *þer* representing the dat. fem. of the article. The line in A would read better with the insertion of this *þer*.

127. B 'His wealth would not be at all the more advanced', i.e. greater.

129. The texts mutually correct each other. The absurd reading *frumþe* (A) is plainly an error for *fremde* (= *fremede*), a stranger; and A supplies the *of* which the Trin. MS. of B omits. 'Except he may make for himself a friend out of a stranger.' In the A.S. version of Matt. xix. 8, where the older MSS. have *frymðe*, i.e. 'beginning', the latest MS. has *fremde*, showing a contrary confusion of the words.

134. A 'Should never a young man be anxious overmuch', i. e. be discouraged; B 'Should never a wise man give himself up to evil'.

136. A 'Though his lot, or state (in life), may not well please him'; B 'Though he may not well like his lot'.

138. 'Nor though he may not control all he would like (to do).'

142. *wowe*, what is amiss; A.S. *wōh*. (Not *woe*.)

143. The readings differ; and both are difficult. A has *Wel is him þat hit·ischapen is*, well is it for him that it (his lot) is predestined. But the line is too long and clumsy. I propose to omit *hit*; 'well for him is that (which) is destined.' We get a still better line by omitting the former *is* also; 'well for him is that destined.' *Schapen* is to destine, to assign as one's lot, to provide, bring it about. Cf. Chaucer's Knight's Tale, A 2541 :—'Wherfore, *to shapen* that they shul not dye.' B has *se* (for *so*) *wel him þet mot scapen*, where the subject of the sentence is *God* (l. 140); and when this is taken as a nominative understood, the sense is—'so well for him may (He) provide that,' viz. good after evil. Morris explains *scapen* by 'escape', which hardly suits. Gropp points out a similar passage in Layamon, ll. 3608–9 :—

> After uvele cumeð god,
> Wel is him þe hit habbe mot!

After evil comes good; well is it for him who may have it.

145. 'It is hard to row against a flowing sea.'

150. Obviously imperfect in both MSS. A is easily put right by inserting *ȝeorne* (eagerly), alliterating with *ȝouhþe* (youth). B has *þe suinch was*, where *suinch* suggests both *swich* and *swinker* (such a toiler); but of course this is only a guess, to stop a gap. Morris suggested *swinker*; but we want *swich* also.

151. B *þanen*, thence, thereby. But possibly wrong. Perhaps read *þanne*, then.

152. Here again a line (or part of one) is lacking in A; but the sense is fairly complete.

154. The reading *edinesse* (prosperity) in B makes better sense than *idelnesse* in A.

155. A 'And also with his worldly wealth please God ere he die'; B 'That he might with his wealth work God's will'.

158. A *bi-towe*; B *bitoȝen*; 'bestowed,' or 'employed.' Both represent A.S. *betogen*, pp. of *betēon*. *Wel bitoȝe*, well employed; Owl and Nightingale, 702. *Uvele bitowen*, ill employed; Ancren Riwle, p. 430.

160. 'Many a man expects—what he ought not to expect—a long life; but that trick deceives him' (B 'will deceive him'). The A.S. verb *wēnan* usually takes after it a *genitive* case, so that the form *lyues* (B *liuis*) is correct, being a survival of the old construction.

It is remarkable that another poem, found in the same MS. as that which affords Text A, seems to have been written upon this very theme, and may have been suggested by lines 160–3. It begins :—

Mon may longe lyues wene,
Ac ofte him lyeþ þe wrench.

It is printed at p. 157 of An Old Eng. Miscellany, ed. Morris, and contains 50 lines.

Yet again, in the Old Kentish Sermons printed in the same volume, at p. 36, we find :—'Man mai longe lyues wene, and ofte him legheth se wrench.' So also in the Ayenbite of Inwyt, ed. Morris, p. 129.

164. A 'For when he has loved his life best of all'; B 'For when he trusts (subj.) in his life best of all'. The text of A cannot be right; *lyues* is caught from l. 162 above, and should rather be *lyf*. And *luuede* should be *luuye*, pres. sing. subjunctive.

167. 'The life (which is) his own.'

168. 'For there is no herb growing (B grown) in wood or in field that can ever uphold the life of the man fated to die' (B 'uphold life'). Here *furþ* = A.S. *ferþ*, *feorþ*, life, soul. It is remarkable that there was a proverb to the contrary, sage being the herb of which the medieval saying ran :—'Cur moriatur homo dum saluia crescit in horto ?'

173. A *heonne turne*, turn hence, i.e. depart, die. B *rimen*, lit. 'make room', i.e. yield his place to others.

177. *doweþes louerd*, Lord of Hosts (Sabaoth). Cf. A.S. *Drihten dugeða waldend*; Judith, l. 61.

182. A *yefst and weldest*, givest away and controllest. There is no difficulty. Morris's correction of *yefst* to *yetst* (gettest?) is not needed.

B *a wold*, in your power, within your control. So in Emare, l. 399 (in Ritson's Metrical Romances, ii. 221), we find :—'His'herte she hadde yn wolde.' And in the Moral Ode, l. 379, where the Jesus Coll. MS. has 'þat alle þinges weldeþ', the Digby MS. (printed by Zupitza in Anglia, vol. i) has 'þet alle þing haueð on wealde' (p. 31).

184. *nywurþe* = *ne ywurþe*, 'become not.' *to wlonk*, 'too proud.'

185. 'Property is not the acquisition of our ancestors, but it is God's gift.' For *lone*, i.e. loan, gift, Wright and Kemble print *loue*, i.e. love. This is entirely wrong, as the reference is to the often quoted passage about poverty upon which I have commented in my Notes to P. Plowman, C. xvii. 117, 136, and to Chaucer, Cant. Tales, D 1195. The passage in P. Plowman says that poverty is 'Cristes owen sonde, *Donum Dei*'. Burton has it, in his Anatomy of Melancholy, Part i. sect. 2. mem. 4. subs. 6. § 1 :—'Poverty, although . . . it be *Donum Dei*, a blessed estate, the way to Heaven, as Chrysostom calls it, God's gift.' And what is true of poverty is equally true of wealth; indeed, the passage in Chrysostom has :—'Diuitiae et paupertas sunt a Domino';

Comment. on Epist. to Hebrews, cap. x. homil. 18. sec. 2 (Migne). Observe the context. Cf. Eccl. v. 19 :—'diuitias .. donum Dei.'

191. 'Then shall our foes seize upon our property.' A *vouh*, evidently an error for *veoh*, A.S. *feoh*; due to the (frequent) miswriting of *e* for *o*. Cf. B *fe.*

193. 'They shall control our treasures, and leave us behind,' i. e. forgotten. B has—'and little bemoan us.' The spelling *Mayþenes* is absurd, but easily corrected from l. 198. *Madmes* is a Norman pronunciation of *maðmes*, 'treasures'; see Layamon, l. 896. It is spelt *maddmess* in the Ormulum, l. 6471. It is the pl. of A.S. *māðum*, *māðm*, a treasure; cf. Goth. *maiþms*, treasure, allied to *maidjan*, to change, Old Lat. *moitāre*, Lat. *mūtāre*, to change; from the notion of exchanging or making a bargain.

196. 'Believe thou not too much upon the sea that flows in,' i. e. in the tide of prosperity.

201. *hit*, sc. thy wealth. *gnyde*, consume, be ground down; an intransitive use of *gnīden*, to rub (Ancren Riwle, p. 238). So in l. 202, *dryue*, lit. 'drive', is used in the sense of 'be driven'.

205. A *vrre*, 'anger'; A.S. *irre*, *ierre*, *yrre*. The form in B is indistinct, but I read it as *erre*, which is quite consistent. Cf. A *hurde*, B *herde*, in l. 10; A.S. *hirde*, *hierde*, *hyrde*.

208. A line seems to be lost, as the metre is imperfect. But I keep to the old numbering of the lines.

211. Gropp (I think rightly) makes a second Part begin here; hence the prefatory address in ll. 212–17. 'Listen ye, my people! Yours is the need; and I will teach you wit and wisdom, that surpass all things.' The correction (in B) of *ou re god* to *ouer-goð* (as in A) is obvious. I note here that *ou re* (B) is really *oure*; it so happens that *ou* ends a line.

218. A 'Secure may he sit, who has him (i. e. wit, *see* l. 221) for a companion'; B 'Secure may he sit, and they who are with him'. B *senden*, 'are'; A.S. *sindon*; as in the Bestiary, ll. 79, 555. Obviously, *hem* must be corrected to *him*. Cf. l. 223.

220. A *a-go*, 'depart'; from A.S. *āgān*, to pass away. B *at-go*, 'depart'; the same sense occurs elsewhere. In Böddeker's Altenglische Dichtungen, p. 188, l. 42, we have—'alle myn godes me at-goht,' all my wealth departs from me; and again, at p. 204, l. 164—'when mi lif is me at-go.' In these cases, *at* has the force of the G. *ent-*; cf. A.S. *æt-flēon*, to flee away, escape, G. *ent-fliehen*.

221. B *went*, 'goes'; *went fro = agoþ* in A.

228. A *arewe*, B *areȝe*. The latter is better. It represents A.S. *earge*, dat. of *earg*, *earh*, inert, cowardly, bad, wicked.' The sense here is 'evil-minded' or 'malicious' man. A 'If thou hast a sorrow, do not

tell it to the malicious; (rather) tell it to thine own saddle-bow, and ride thee on, singing. Then will he, who does not know thy lot, suppose that thy lot well pleases thee.' Here 'tell it to your saddle-bow' simply means—'keep it to yourself.' *þin* (B) is for *þen* = *þan* (A).

235. A 'If thou hast a sorrow, and the malicious man knows it, he will bemoan thee to thy face, but behind, he will blame (B deride) thee'.

239. 'Thou mightest say it to such a man, that he very well wishes it for thee.' Here *on* = A.S. *ann*, used as the pres. sing. of *unnan*, to grant, to wish (something for a person), to like (one to have something); see *unnan* in Toller.

241. A 'Without any pity he wishes thee much more'; B 'Thou mayst tell thy grief to such a one as would wish that thou haddest more (of it)'.

echere is the dat. fem. of *ech*, each, any.

249. *by hire wlyte*, by her face, for her beauty.

250. It is necessary to supply *hire* in B; the sense is—'nor bring her to thy dwelling for the sake of any wealth (of hers).' *Bury* is hardly the right word; *bure*, dat. of *bur*, a bower, a bridal-chamber, seems better; see l. 309.

252. A 'But learn her virtues; she will show them very soon'. *Custe* is the A.S. *cysta*, pl. of *cyst*, fem.

B is imperfect; I restore it as well as I can. 'Ere thou learn her virtues that she may show.'

254. 'For many a man, for wealth's sake, reckons (B hastens) amiss.' Cf. A.S. *ge-eahtian*, to estimate, to value (Toller).

256. A 'And often a man, of a fair one, chooses a base one'. *Frakel* is a variant of A.S. *fracoð*, *fracod*, vile. In Old Eng. Homilies, ed. Morris, i. 24, we find mention of an apple that is 'wið-uten feire, and *frakel* wið-innen', i. e. fair outside, and rotten inside. And see l. 349. Both here and in l. 349 B has the form *fokel*, which must be taken as a variant of *foken*, though it looks like a modification of the latter due to association with *frakel*. *Foken* means 'fraudulent' or 'fickle', and is from the same root as *fickle*; the Teutonic base *fīk-, to deceive, giving a strong grade *fāk- (M.E. *fōk-) and a weak grade *fik-. The Ormulum has 'fakenn trowwþe', deceitful faith, l. 12655. And Robert of Brunne, ed. Hearne, p. 194, has 'Saladyn was fulle *focn*', Saladin was very deceitful.

262. Note the use of *he* = he (A); *he* = she (B).

264. See Zupitza's note, quoted near the end of the Introduction, § 41.

271. *þu*, thou, is understood; 'that ever (thou) may say to thy wife all thy desire.' *Segge* (A) = A.S. *secge*, thou may say, 2 p. s. pres.

subjunctive. By comparing the form *sai* (B) with the form *siȝe* in B 480, we obtain the correct spelling *saiȝe* for this text.

273. A 'For if she saw all thy foes before thee, and thou hadst made her wrath by a word, she would never desist (lit. let it go), for any living thing, (so) that she would not upbraid thee continually for thy times of adversity. Woman is word-mad, and has a tongue too swift; though she might well wish it, she can in no way control it.'

290. 'That light misdemeanour she might give up, if she were often overtoiled in sweat; though it is difficult to bend that which does not wish to be true.' B has—'If she, overtoiled, were covered with sweat as she never thought (to be).'

294. B *ac þoh*, but nevertheless.

295. A *treowe*, true, straight, upright, &c. B has *ter*, which is mis-written for the same word. Kemble hesitated over the word, as to whether it was *ter* or *tre*, and finally gave it as *ter tre* (two words); Wright had turned it into the form *tertre*! Kemble explains the B-text thus: 'yet it is evil to cultivate that which a tree will not become,' i.e. that which will not become a tree. But 'bewen' (probably an error for 'beȝen') is the A.S. *býgan*, to incline or bend, and not A.S. *búan*, to cultivate. I do not think there is any reference to the actual word *tree*, though the image may well be that of inclining a growing tree to exhibit a perfectly straight and upright stem. There is no real contradiction in such a phrase as 'to bend straight'; it is in constant use. The N.E.D., s. v. *bend*, 7 b, quotes from R. C., Time's Whistle (1616), ed. 1871, 125 :—

> The tree growing crooked, if you'l have it mended,
> Whilst that it is a twigg, it must be bended.

The wilful woman is not one who objects to being a tree (i.e. to growing up), but to being a *straight* tree.

296. 'For the cat often catches mice in the same way as her mother.'

300. A 'He shall never be heard (to be) master of his word; but she shall sternly torment and vex him; and seldom shall he be blithe and glad, the man that is his wife's aversion'.

302. B 'But she shall raise (provide) for him tediousness [better *treiȝe*, affliction], and many a vexation (shall he) strangely have. Seldom shall he be in happiness.' The wording of B is suspicious.

306. Cf. note above, to l. 256.

306*. B *on leme*, 'in the sunbeam'; not 'in its look', as in Kemble. In fact, the James MS. has *beme*.

311. *and þeyh*, and nevertheless. B has an extra line.

315. I can make nothing of *werȝe*, the form in Wright and Kemble. But I read the word as *weiȝe*, a variant of *weȝe*; 'proud on the highway,' i. e. conspicuous in public.

315. A *bi þe glede*, beside the glowing coal, i. e. by the fireside.

316. Morris explains *wike* (B) by 'war'; but this requires the form *wige*. *Wike* may stand, as it means 'office'. Then the sense is—'proud on the highway, but worthless in an office (of trust)'.

318. B has *Aretu*; and, comparing *Aretu noht* with the reading *Neure þu .. ne arede* in A, it becomes obvious that *Aretu* is merely a contraction of *Ared-tu*, for *Ared þu*. The final *-e* in *arede* (A) is correct, and is due to the position of the words. In *ared-tu, ared* is the second person imperative; but in *neure þu ne arede, arede* is in the subjunctive mood. A 'Never do thou, in thy life, too seriously take as your counsel the word of thy wife. If she be angered by word or deed, a woman weeps for temper, oftener than for any good; and often, in all cases, in order to further her will.'

323. All three editions have *fro* (B); but the MS. has *for* (correctly).

325. *lude and stille*, 'loudly and silently'; a common adverbial expression, meaning 'under all circumstances'; as in l. 439. Thus in Barbour's Bruce, iii. 745:—

> That thai and thairis, *loud and still*,
> Suld be in all thing at his will.

Two examples, from MSS., are given in Halliwell's Dictionary.

329. *Salomon*, Solomon; see the Vulgate version. But I doubt if the alleged sentence is in Solomon's Proverbs. The reference is perhaps to Publilius Syrus, Sent. 324:—'Malo in consilio feminae uincunt uiros'; alluded to in Chaucer's Melibeus, B. 2253, where this saying is attributed to 'the philosophre'; see my Note on the passage.

331. A 'He who follows her counsel, she brings him to sorrow.'

333. A *loþ* (*sic* in MS.); evidently an error for *leoþ*, 'a song.' It then rhymes with *forteoþ*. B (l. 335) has *in lede* (James MS.—*in þe led*), which likewise means 'in the song'; the spelling *led* occurs in Genesis and Exodus, ed. Morris, l. 27:—'Bidde ic singen non oðer *lēd*.' The spelling *leoð* occurs in Layamon, and in Old Eng. Homilies, ed. Morris, ii. 163, l. 20; ii. 213, l. 16.

334. Unfortunately we do not know the song whence this is quoted, or the relevancy of the quotation would be more apparent. However, the reference must be to women, and the literal sense of this line (which is not in B) is:—'like twilight-shadows, (they) mislead (us).' *Scūm* (or *scūme*) is the Icel. *skūmi*, dusk, twilight. The N.E.D., s.v. *fortee*, quotes the passage, and explains *forteoþ* as 'draw away [to evil], seduce'; but says nothing as to *scumes*.

335. *ifurn*, 'of old time'; A.S. *gefyrn*.

336. Chaucer makes Chanticleer quote this proverb:—'Wommannes counseils been ful ofte colde'; Cant. Tales, B. 4446. It will be found in the Icelandic Dictionary, s. v. *kaldr*:—'Köld eru opt kvenna-rāð,' cold

·[fatal] are oft women's counsels. In the Tale of Melibeus, B. 2286, the corresponding Latin text has: 'uulgo dici consueuit, Consilium feminile nimis carum aut nimis uile.'

337. *unlěde*, miserable, wretched; A.S. *unlæde*, *unlæd*, Goth. *unlěds*, poor. Lit. 'landless', and allied to Icel. *lǎð*, land, landed property, Gk. λήιον, a crop, a cornfield; cf. ἀλήϊos, poor, Iliad, ix. 125; πολυλήϊos, with many cornfields, Iliad, v. 613.

339. *Ne .. nouht* is equivalent to a single negative. 'I do not say this because a good woman is not a good thing.' We must certainly read *nys* (*ne is*, is not) in l. 340. In A the letter *n* has been erased before *ys*; no doubt the double negative in l. 339 caused some confusion in the scribe's mind. We have the phrase again in l. 707, where *ne ben* is quite clear and correct:—'I do not say (it) because many (such a one) is not a gentleman.'

341. *þe mon* is practically a dative; 'for the man that may choose her, and gain (her) over others,' i.e. as against other wooers. B 'for the man that might know her and choose her from (among) others'. The M.E. *coueren* (*coveren*) often means to gain or obtain; in the Cursor Mundi, l. 964, the Trinity MS. has *gete* (get, obtain), where the Cotton MS. has *couer*; see *Cover*, vb. (2) in N.E.D.

344, 345. Repeated from ll. 160, 161.

346. 'That he has a friend, where one promises him fairly, (and) speaks him fairly to his face, and evilly behind his back.' In l. 347 *me* is an attenuated form of *man* (see *mon* in B), and is used just like the modern E. *one*, or the modern G. *man*, or the F. *on* (i.e. L. *homo*). So again in l. 350.

350. A 'So (*or*, in this way) one may longest lead (draw after one) the hostile one'; i.e. this is how to keep an enemy on one's own side longest, viz. by fair words. B 'Thus one may longest retain wealth'.

352. B *gin þu leuen*, do thou believe. *Gin*, lit. 'begin', is here a mere auxiliary verb, like *do*.

356. A 'Many a man has a deceitful mouth, (is) mild, and (yet) very wicked to (other) men; he will not let thee know when he will entrap thee'; B 'For many a man has a deceitful mind, and he is (apparently) friendly to men; thou shalt never know', &c.

In B we must take *cuð* in the sense of 'friendly', as Kemble does; see *Couth* in N.E.D. In both texts *monne* represents the A.S. *mannum*, dat. plural.

In A *forcuþ* has the usual sense of 'very wicked' or 'infamous'. As noted in N.E.D., the A.S. form was *forcúð*, with the stress on the second element, and thus exactly equivalent to Goth. *frakunths*, pp. of *frakunnan*, to despise, to know to be bad. The word must also (in the prehistoric period) have sometimes been used with a stress on the former element, which produced the A.S. forms *frácoþ, frácod, fráced,* with the same sense of 'infamous'. In the M.E. period, the form *forcuð* likewise had the accent on the former syllable, as here; the line is to be scanned:—' míld' and mónne fór-cuþ.' The same accentuation occurs in Layamon, l. 28240:—'Nu wás som fórcuð kémpe.'

361. A *sawe*; B *saʒe*. Both represent the A.S. *sagu,* a saw, saying, proverb. 'Proverbs make a man wise.'

362. A *i-sēlþe*; B *sēlþe*; 'prosperity.' From the A.S. *sǣlþe,* prosperity, good fortune; allied to *sǣl,* a fit time, opportunity, luck, happiness, and Goth. *sēls,* adj., fortunate. 'Good luck makes a man prudent.'

363. 'Through lying a man becomes hated, and through evil tricks (he becomes) worthless.'

365. The words *þat he bereþ* form a gloss, and should be struck out. A 'And by means of (his) hooked (i.e. thievish) hands [that he possesses] he ruins himself'; B 'And hooked hands make the man lose his head'. The line in A is to be scanned—And þúrh hóked' hónde.

367. A 'Accustom thyself (to refrain) from lying.'

369. Tautological; *on þeode* and *in alle leode* are equivalent. 'So might thou in public be beloved in every company.'

379. A *lond le*; a mere scribal error for *londe* (as in B); Gropp's note.

384. A 'And treasures of each (i.e. every) kind'. Here *vy* (in *vyches*) is for *uy* = *ui,* variant of *ue* = *eu*; both *ue* and *eu* were used to represent the F. *eu* in *peuple,* a sound that is sometimes found in the old forms of 'each'. See *aighwilc* in Stratmann, who notes the spelling *euch* in St. Katharine, the Ancren Riwle, and the Owl and Nightingale. In a poem on Doomsday, l. 4, pr. in Morris's Old Eng. Miscellany, p. 162, one MS. has *euch* where the other (the Jesus Coll. MS.) has *vych.*

386. *ure* (A), 'our.' The reading *wure* in B may be meant for *ʒure,* 'your'; but *ure* is better. See l. 401.

399. A 'Christ's will'; B 'what is pleasing to Christ'.

400*. B *þe wis* (MS. þe uuíſ); printed *we mus* (!) in Kemble and Wright; though the *uu* is quite clear, and the *i* is distinctly marked. 'Therefore let us bethink ourselves to lead our life in that wise that God doth instruct us.' The text is imperfect. Gropp rightly corrects the old reading *leten* (in B 402) to *leren* (as in A); for in fact *leren* is the actual reading in the Trinity MS., for which both Kemble and Wright substituted *leten,* which only makes nonsense.

405*. In B, read *Salomon þe wise,* for the metre. It is a more natural order of the words. The scribe of A, finding the word *Salomon* thus repeated, obviously thought that such repetition was unintentional, and wrote it but *once.*

407. A *lyen,* 'loan,' i.e. reward; a rare spelling of M.E. *lēan,* A.S. *lēan*; cf. Goth. *laun,* reward. In the Moral Ode, pr. in Morris's Specimens of

E. Eng., two MSS. have *lean* (l. 65); but the Egerton MS. has *lyen*, as printed in Early Eng. Poems and Lives of Saints, ed. Furnivall, p. 24, couplet 32. Perhaps the saying of Solomon here alluded to is that in Prov. xi. 18, or xxiv. 14. The text in B cannot be right, as *hit* in l. 409 refers to *lyen*, which is not there! Gropp corrects *is boþ* (B) to *beþ*, and rightly. But we must further correct *doþ* in l. 406 to *deþ*, as in A. The lines then rime.

420. 'Can well include much.'

426. The A.S. *tunge* is feminine. Thus *heo* (A) and *he* (B) both mean 'she'.

428. Cf. Prov. xxiii. 24.

438. A *werende*; read *wexende* (Morris); see l. 433. A 'But if thou lettest him exercise his own will on all occasions, while he is growing up in the world, thou wilt not be able to control him', &c.

445. A 'he will disregard thy command'. Cf. B 446.

453. A *arixlye*, rule, have the mastery. From M.E. *rixlien*, to rule (Stratmann); formed from A.S. *ricsian*, to rule.

454. A 'so that he may not (be able to) get at it', i.e. control it. See *Areach* in N.E.D.

NB. The colophon in A—*Expliciunt, &c.*—is counted as l. 457 in Morris's edition (and here).

459. 'To be well drunk or without drink, either (state) is very good wisdom; no man need drink the less, when (i. e. whilst) he be wise therewithal'; i. e. as long as he has complete control of himself.

469. 'Sorrow sucketh to him (i.e. soaks into him) as salt does in meat, sucks (soaks) through his body as blood does through the body; and his morrow-sleep (next morning's sleep) shall be long-lasting, whosoever hath thus evilly drunk on the evening (before).' Evidently *werse* in l. 475 should be *hwoso*; and *þe* = that.

474. For *lestin* we must certainly read *lestinde*, as all the present participles end in *-inde* or *-ende* in both texts. In fact, after *lestin*, there is a trace of an erased *d*.

480. For the construction, cf. l. 271, and the note.

487. *loþe*, loathed, disliked; Kemble's suggestion.

492. 'For when the mouth babbles,' &c.

495. Read *eft*, again (Morris). It seems to mean that the enemy (once a friend) may have heard of a thing once and have forgotten it; and then a too talkative person may remind him of it again. Literally—'then will his ears hear it again.'

497. 'If thou gain a friend by thy liberally-bestowed wealth.'

500. The MS. has *þeuues þines*; but grammar requires the form *þine* (dat. pl.), as possessive pronouns are declined like adjectives. The *s* has been added by the influence of *þeuues* = *þewes*, i.e. virtues, good qualities.

509. 'Then shalt thou be alone as thou wast before.'

513. 'Better would it be for thee.'

516. Here *duȝe* (in the Trinity MS.) is an error for *duȝeðe* (as in the James MS.); see l. 544. Pronounced *duȝþe*, as a disyllable; for the form *duhþe*, see Stratmann. For the spelling *duþe*, see O. Eng. Miscellany, ed. Morris, p. 91, l. 15.

517. *senden* (Trin MS.); an error for *sendeþ* (as in the James MS.). Supply *it* from the James MS. Gropp notes: 'I believe that *senden* is the 3 s. pres. subj. of *senden*, to send. The object of this verb is *duge* (wealth) in the for[e]going line, so that the meaning of the passage is: '"And God send thee wealth."' But he forgot that the 3 s. pres. subj. is *sende*. Fortunately, the James MS. is correct.

520. *faires*, 'goods'; Morris. Both transcripts agree here. A very unusual sense, but not impossible. The A.S. *fæger*, sb., meant 'beauty'; and the N.E.D. gives:—'Fair, adj.; B. sb.² sense 4, beauty, fairness, good looks. Also *pl.* points or traits of beauty (obsolete).' Perhaps we may translate it by 'fine things'. Kemble suggests *feres*, 'companions'; which does not suit the context.

525. *letet* = *let it*, let it alone, disregard it. MS. J has *lef it*, 'believe it'; which is better.

526. Printed by Wright and Morris as one line, but by Kemble as two (rightly). I count it as one, to preserve the old numbering.

529. 'So that he will not hear (any one) mention thee by word of mouth, but he will always be sorry when he thinks of thee.' I supply *þe*, thee; MS. J has *te*. In l. 532, MS. J. supplies *of*.

534. *to tune*, 'among us.' This is a common adverbial phrase; lit. 'to the town', i.e. to the place where we live. But it came to mean no more than 'among us', without any further note of locality. See the examples in Toller. In the Menologium or A.S. Poetical Calendar, the month of March is said to come in 'us to tune', i.e. among us. Lye, in his A.S. Dictionary, explains it by 'in turn', but this sense is not so well borne out. It occurs in Middle English also. Thus 'Lenten ys come wiþ loue *to toune*' simply means that 'the spring has come among us lovingly'; see Spec. of English, ed. Morris and Skeat, Part II, p. 48.

544. 'Do thou distribute thy wealth to thy dear friends.' *Frende* is dat. pl.; A.S. *frēondum*. Cf. *monne*, dat. pl. in l. 357.

548. 'Put no trust in those who remain after thee.'

554. 'For he that is shut out is soon forgotten within.' Out of sight, out of mind.

559. 'And thou canst not guide thyself by devices of any kind.' *None cunnes* (usually *nones cunnes*) is the gen. sing.

564. 'For all His gift'; for all He has given thee. The reading

loue (love) is improbable, as the last syllable in the line but one is usually long and strongly dwelt upon.

þanke of, i. e. thank *for*; the usual old idiom, and common; see Chaucer's Truth, l. 19.

571. The long poem known as Layamon's Brut ends with the very same couplet, viz.—'iwurðe þet iwurðe . iwurðe Godes wille!' I. e. 'let happen what may, God's will be done.' The direction in l. 570, viz. 'say thou, *at the end*', shows that an explicit reference to that work is here intended. Moreover, Part II ends exactly *here*, and the poem once ended here also; see note to l. 573.

573. A third Part begins here. Each of the sections in this part (except 35–37) begins with an address to the speaker's *son*.

579. 'That my hair grows pale (or white).' The verb *to fallow*, to wither, grow pale, could be applied to the hair; see N.E.D. Both Wright and Kemble misprinted *her* as *hert*, but that means 'a hart'. *Herte*, 'heart,' is disyllabic, and occurs in l. 581. Morris conjectured *hew*, 'hue'; but the MS. is correct. The idea of 'hue' is represented by *wlite* in l. 580.

582. *dōn-e* (disyllabic), 'done,' i. e. ended; pp. treated as an adj. pl.

583. Note *unc*, the dual form. 'And we must divide us two,' i. e. part one from the other.

589. *barin*, for *barn*, 'bairn,' child; cf. l. 625. The spelling denotes a strong trill of the *r*, and the word, for a metrical purpose, is disyllabic.

592. *wið child*, towards, or to (each) child. It was said of Arthur, that ' he wes þan ȝungen for fader, þan alden for frouer'; Layamon's Brut, l. 19936.

594, 595, 596. Grammatically, *gin* is the right form, as it is a strong verb, and precedes the pronoun. It is also more correct metrically.

598..' And, son, conduct thyself according to law, and the Lord shall love thee.'

601. 'God be to thee fully in (thy) memory.' The insertion of *in* is necessary both for the sense and the metre.

604. Kemble inserts *he* as if it were in the MS. But it is not there, though obviously required.

611. 'Then shall all the people love thee.' In Layamon, both *leoden* and *leodes* occur as the pl. of *leod*.

613. 'To the young man give thou law; let the old man have his land.' The MS. has *þad helde*, against grammar. Read *þan*, 'the,' masc. accusative. Cf. ll. 350, 352, 627.

617. *rēme* can only represent the A.S. verb *rȳman*, to make room; it cannot possibly represent A.S. *rūm*, sb. or adj. The line is awkward; we must take *þu ȝef* by itself, as 'do thou grant'. The sense is :—'do

thou permit him to clear the way, i. e. to have plenty of room.   If this be right, read *wei* rather than *weie*.

621. *bus*; for this Morris proposes to read *buȝe*, i. e. bow aside, avoid; but this is quite at variance with the context.   The form is correct; it is the contracted form of *buȝes*, 2nd pers. sing. indic., used as a future; 'thou shalt bow.'   It is noted in the N.E.D., s.v. *Bow*, vb. 2 b., that *bow* can be used in a wide sense, 'to bend one's course, to turn or direct one's steps, wend one's way, make one's way, go, betake oneself.'   Most often, it means (in such a case) to turn to flee; but it is occasionally used of a bold advance.   Thus, in Layamon, l. 5559, we read that the Romans retreated because they saw Brennus '*buȝe heom to-ȝeines*', i. e. advance (threateningly) towards them.   This is the case here also.   The sense is :—'Son, thou wilt best advance towards the foolish man of abusive speech, and beat him afterwards therewith (at the time), that he may begin to smart'; lit. 'that it may begin to smart to him'.   I supply *to* for the metre as well as for the sense.   Cf. l. 629.   Thus *bus to* is like the modern slang phrase 'go for'.

627. *beuir hore*, 'trembling hoary-headed man' (Morris).   Cf. A.S. *bifian* (G. *beben*), to tremble; whence an adj. **bif-or* might have been formed, like *wac-or*, wakeful, from *wac-an*, to wake.   Cf. prov. E. *bever*, sb. a tremor; vb. to shake (E.D.D.).   The adjective is not otherwise known.   The reference is obviously to Levit. xix. 32—'Coram cano capite consurge'; to which Chaucer also alludes in his Pardoneres Tale, C. 743.

629. *buh þe*, bow thyself, advance; see note to l. 621.

633. Obviously *wite*, A.S. *wita*, 'wise man,' is the right word here. Kemble takes it to mean—'well be with thee'; but this makes nonsense of the next line.   It means—'Well be it with the wise man who first taught thee.'

641. 'For one may outride the older man better than (one can) surpass him in counsel.'   See remarks on this below; p. 73.

645. 'Choose thou never, for a companion, the evil, listening man,' the eaves-dropper.   See *Listening*, pres. part., and *Listen*, in N.E.D. The form *lusninde* is right; cf. A.S. *hlosnian*, to listen (Toller), *hlysnan*, to listen, O.E. Texts, ed. Sweet, p. 567, and O. Northumb. *lysnas*, as a gloss to Lat. *audite*, in Matt. xiii. 18.   Cf. l. 654.

648. 'From the mad man thou mayest make thy way (escape) by wiles and by weapons; but, when thou least expectest it, the evil man will deceive thee.   The bitch bites severely, though she barks quietly; so doth the listening evil man often, when he dare do it.'

656. 'When he is outwardly still, he bites badly in secret.'

658. *bi-fuliþ*, befouls, covers with dirt.

659. 'When he unfolds himself'; Kemble.   But this makes no sense

at all; and Morris's Glossary omits *vnfoldith*. The solution is easy; for *vnfoldith* is merely a careless variant of *umfoldith*, i. e. folds round, embraces. 'He wholly befouls his friend, when he embraces him'; which is graphic enough. The pp. *umfaldin*, enclosed, occurs in The Wars of Alexander, ed. Skeat, 4717. In the same, l. 2134, we find *vmlapis*, 'encompasses,' which, in l. 1932, is misspelt *vnlappis*; and there are other examples of this confusion.

663. 'The scornful, lying man.'

665. *keren*. It cannot mean 'turn', as Kemble suggests, for that verb was palatalised to *cherren*. Nor can it represent M.E. *cairen*, to go, as that is spelt with *ai*. As the *k*-sound remains, it follows that *e* represents (as it may in the Southern dialect) the A.S. *y*; and *keren* is the M.E. *cüren* (Stratmann), to choose, a verb formed from A.S. *cyre*, choice. The sense is:—'he will steal thy goods and choose (from them), and will cunningly make answer (about them)'; i. e. he will pick and steal what he most wants, and then appear quite innocent.

Two examples of M.E. *cüren* are known; in the Ancren Riwle, p. 56, note *l*, *icured* is a variant of *ichosen* (chosen); and in St. Katharine, l. 1870, the Lat. *eligere* is translated by *curen and cheosen*, i. e. select and choose.

670. Something is lost, as the metre goes wrong. Morris prints it thus:—

> and oþer he wole liþen and hokerful ben,
> þuru hoker *and* lesing þe aloþed.

We want some such arrangement as the following:—

> and oþer he wole liȝen
> and hokerful ben [*euere*,
> *oþer lihtliche biswiken*
> *and harmen þe*]; þoru hoker
> and lesing, &c.

The sense being:—'and either he will lie, and [*ever*] be scornful, [*or easily deceive and harm thee*]; by (his) scorn and lying all men that know him will loathe thee.' But we can only guess. The excellent correction of *liþen* to *liȝen* (670) is due to Gropp.

673. 'But take to thee a steadfast man, who can employ both word and deed and multiply your property; such a companion is a help in need.' Though Kemble reads *mod*, he explains it as *niod* 'need', as 'help in need' is a common phrase, and *mod* (mood, courage) gives little sense, though it yields a perfect rime. The MS. has 'mode' or 'moð', the *d* being followed by an upward curl.

679. 'Never choose for companion a little man, a tall man, or a red man.' See below, ll. 682, 692, 702.

682. *rei*, for *reih*, *reh*, A.S. *hrēoh*, 'fierce.'   So also *nei* for *neih*, 'nigh,' in l. 683.

684, 685. Kemble and Wright end these lines with *teir* and *beir* (no sense), which Morris altered to *bere* and *tere* (uselessly).   However, the MS. rightly has *ten* and *ben* (A.S. *tēon* and *bēon*).   'He will conduct himself (as being) so worthy, that he would fain be his lord's master.' Cf. *ðat he sulde him ten*, 'that they should conduct themselves'; Genesis and Exodus, 1913.

686. 'Unless he may show himself off proudly, he will make unpleasant noises.   He will grin, and fight (or swagger), and chide, and ever go about with disturbing noises.'   *luden* answers to a pl. of A.S. *hlȳd*, a loud noise, clamour, allied to *hlūd*, loud.   *cocken* is to behave like a cock, to fight, to swagger, to strut.   In *vn-luden*, the prefix *vn-* (= *un-*) has a sinister signification, as in A.S. *un-þēaw*, a bad habit, *un-tīma*, an unfit time.

692. *leþe-bei*, supple-jointed; A.S. *leoðu-bīge*; from A.S. *leoðu-*, allied to *lið*, a joint, and *bīgan*, *bȳgan*, to cause to bend, causal of *būgan*, to bow.   Cf. *þine leoðebeie limen*, thy supple-jointed limbs; St. Marherete, p. 16, l. 17.   See *Litheby* in N.E.D.

696. *bi forð daȝes*, by the advance of the day, late in the day, in the twilight of evening.   A curious idiom; see *Forth*, 4 b, in N.E.D. Compare, says Gropp, Wyclif, Mark vi. 35; *whanne it was forth daies*, when it was late in the day.

697. *in huge werd*, in a large crowd (of people); A.S. *werod*.

699. *he þewiþ ut*, he shouts out.   The verb does not occur elsewhere, and is probably imitative, like the A.S. *þēotan*, to howl.   Cf. prov. E. *thew*, to threaten; Cornwall; E.D.D.

700. 'If he slides into a ditch, he is dead for a certainty.'

702. 'The red man, he is a devil; for he will advise thee (to) thine ill.'

706. We have here the same construction as in l. 339 above (see note to that line).   'I do not say this because many a man is not a gentleman'; i.e. I admit that many men are such.

708. It is remarkable that these last two lines contain *four* French words; for they are very scarce throughout the poem.   Not only do we find *genteleri* in l. 708, but the three concluding words of the poem are all alike of French origin.

NOTES ON THE PROVERBS

(The numbers refer to the Sections. For the Proverbs of Hending, see Altenglische Dichtungen, ed. K. Böddeker, Berlin, 1878. The references to ' D.' are to Sprichwörter der germanischen und romanischen Sprachen, von Ida von Düringsfeld, Leipzig, 1872, vol. i. Those to ' D. ii.' are to the same, vol. ii.)

1. Introductory. With respect to Alfred, see the Preface.

2. This is practically an expansion of the first of the Ten Commandments.

3. Pieces concerning the duties of a king are fairly common. See one in Anglo-Saxon, printed from MS. Cotton, Nero A 1, fol. 71, in a note at p. 363 of Political Poems and Songs, ed. T. Wright (Camden Soc.). Also the note in Warton's Hist. of Eng. Poetry, ed. 1840, ii. 231, upon the Secretum Secretorum Aristotelis, addressed (under the name of Aristotle), to Alexander the Great; of which considerable use was made by Gower, Hoccleve, and Lydgate. Hoccleve's poem De Regimine Principum is founded upon it. Cf. Piers Plowman, B-text, prol. 128, and the note. Also Wisdom, x. 1–6; Ecclus. x. 1, 2; &c.

4, 5. See the duty of the *Bellatores*, or knights, in the A.S. piece mentioned just above; also Ælfric's Saints' Lives, ed. Skeat, ii. 121; P. Plowman, B. vi. 22–56; Gower, Conf. Amantis, bk. viii. 3021, &c.; Wyclif's Works, ed. Arnold, iii. 206.

4, l. 82. From Galat. vi. 7. Cf. Owl and Nightingale, 1037–8; D. ii. 649.

A. 6. See Proverbs of Hending, st. 3, and st. 6. Cf. Chaucer, Book of the Duchesse, 791–2; Roman de la Rose, ed. Méon, l. 13094; Horace, Epist. i. 2. 69. Kemble (p. 281) quotes the medieval proverb :—Quod puer adsuescit, leviter dimittere nescit. Cf. Prov. xxii. 6; Ecclus. vi. 18; D. 845, 847.

A. 7. ' How much better it is to get wisdom than gold,' &c.; Prov. xvi. 16. Cf. Prov. xxii. 1.

A. 8. A recommendation to patience. Cf. Owl and Nightingale, 687, 689; Prov. of Hending, st. 23.

A. 9. Kemble quotes from Piers of Fulham, ll. 303–4, as printed in Hazlitt's Early Popular Poetry, ii. 13 :—

> Hard it is to stryve with wynde or wawe,
> Whether it do ebbe or flowe.

Also from Skelton's Works, p. 54 :—' He is nat wise agayne the stream

that striueth'; see his Garlande of Laurell, l. 1432.   And he refers to
Howell, Eng. Prov. pp. 9, 11; Adagia, p. 30; Gartner, Dict. 28, 36 *b*.
' It is hard striving against the stream'; Camden's Remaines.—Hazlitt's
Proverbs.   See D. 849; D. ii. 104, 407.

A. 10. Cf. Prov. of Hending, st. 39.   As to l. 168, see Kemble's
note (at p. 252).   He quotes, e. g. the German proverb—' Es wechst
kein kraut für den todt im garten'; Grüter, Prov. Alem. p. 39.   Cf.
D. ii. 460.   And see notes above, to ll. 160, 168; pp. 57, 58.

A. 11. ' Noli anxius esse in diuitiis iniustis,' &c.; Ecclus. v. 10 (v. 8
in A.V.).   ' Est qui locupletatur parce agendo . . . et nescit quod . . .
relinquat omnia aliis, et morietur'; Ecclus. xi. 18–20.   Cf. Prov. xi.
4, 28; D. ii. 374, 524.

A. 12. Cf. Psalm lxii. 10; Luke xii. 15.   ' Better God than gold';
Hazlitt.   See D. 210.

A. 13. Cf. Prov. xxii. 1.   See Prov. of Hending, st. 3; D. ii. 231.

A. 14. See Prov. of Hending, st. 12.   Cf. Ecclus. viii. 19; xi. 29;
xii. 10; D. 554.

A. 15. See Prov. of Hending, st. 17, 18, and st. 36.   Cf. Ecclus.
xlii. 12–14; D. 338; D. ii. 325.

A. 16. Cf. Prov. xxi. 19; xxv. 24.

A. 17. ' That that comes of a cat will catch mice'; Ray's Proverbs.
He quotes the Italian equivalent.   See Kemble, who also quotes (at
p. 253) :—' Prendere maternam bene discit cattula praedam'; &c.   Cf.
D. 879.

A. 17, l. 306.   Cf. ' al swa is an eppel . . wið-uten feire and frakel
wið-innen'; Old Eng. Homilies, ed. Morris, i. 25.   See Chaucer,
Cant. Tales, G 964–5; and my note, vol. v. p. 428.   Cf. D. 107.

A. 18. See Chaucer, Cant. Tales, B 4446; and my note, vol. v.
p. 255.   Cf. Ecclus. xxv. 23; xxvi. 7; D. 486.

A. 19. See Ecclus. vi. 9; xi. 33; D. 497.

A. 20. See Prov. i. 1–6; Ecclus. xii. 21, 22; xxxix. 1–3; Levit.
xix. 18; D. ii. 521.

A. 21. See Ps. xxxix. 6; lxii. 10; Prov. xi. 4; xxvii. 24.

l. 406. Cf. Wisdom, v. 15; iii. 5; Eccles. viii. 12; Ps. xxxvii. 37.

A. 22. Cf. Ecclus viii. 3, 11, 16, 19; Prov. x. 19.

l. 419. Cf. Ecclus. xxxii. 8.

l. 421. Cf. Prov. xii. 16; Prov. of Hending, st. 11; and see Shak.
Hen. V, iii. 7. 132; As You Like It, v. 4. 67.   Kemble quotes from
MS. Harl. 3362, fol. 4 :—' Ut dicunt multi, cito transit lancea stulti.'
And see Chaucer, Parl. of Foules, 574, and the note.

l. 425. ' The stroke of the tongue breaketh the bones'; Ecclus.
xxviii. 17.   ' A soft tongue breaketh the bone'; Prov. xxv. 15.   See
Owl and Night., 297; Prov. of Hending, st. 19.   ' Osse caret lingua,

secat os tamen ipsa maligna'; a medieval proverb, quoted in P. Piper, Die älteste deutsche Litteratur, Berlin (1884), p. 278. And see Skelton, ed. Dyce, i. 134; D. ii. 744.

A. 23. Prov. x. 1; xxiii. 24; Ecclus. xxx. 9. Cf. Prov. of Hending, st. 5, st. 6, and st. 9; D. 475.

l. 451. Prov. xiii. 24; Ecclus. xxx. 1.

B. 15. See Ecclus. xxxi. 27; Prov. of Hending, st. 38; D. 554.

B. 18. Cf. Prov. xvii. 27; x. 19. See Notes to Chaucer, vol. v. pp. 442-3.

B. 22. Prov. xviii. 24; vi. 3; xvii. 17; xix. 6; xxvii. 9, 10, 17; Ecclus. ix. 10; xxxvii. 6.

B. 24. Cf. Prov. of Hending, st. 13 and st. 16.

B. 27. l. 544. Cf. Prov. of Hending, st. 27; and the modern proverb—'out of sight, out of mind.' See Notes to Chaucer, Cant. Tales, A 3392; in vol. v. 105.

B. 28. Cf. Ecclus. ii. 4; D. 547-550. An exhortation to resignation. It is remarkable that ll. 571-2 coincide with the last two lines in Layamon's Brut, as already noted.

B. 30. The last six sections form a distinct Part; and resemble the similar pieces of advice with such titles as 'A Father's Instructions,'[1] 'How the Wise Man taught his Son,' and 'How the Good Wife taught her Daughter'; see vol. i. of Hazlitt's Early Popular Poetry; and cf. Notes to Chaucer, Cant. Tales, H 317; vol. v. p. 442. See Prov. i. 8: ii. 1; iii. 1, &c.; Ecclus. ii. 1; iii. 1, &c. Cf. D. 74, 82.

l. 592. Cf. Ecclus. iv. 10.

l. 635. Cf. Ecclus. vi. 34, 35.

l. 641. See Chaucer, Troil. iv. 1456; Cant. Tales, A 2449; Salomon and Saturn, ed. Kemble, p. 253; Owl and Night., l. 762.

l. 652. Kemble (p. 254) quotes the proverb—'Great barkers are not biters'; and the like. He refers to Greene's play of George a Greene; see Act iv. sc. 3 (ed. Collins, l. 903, and the note).

l. 680. Kemble (p. 254) notes that similar warnings against short, tall, and red men occur in German and medieval Latin. He observes :— 'The faithlessness of red-haired men is known to have been a widely prevailing belief, and to have passed into the proverbs of many European countries: Judas, 'in the painted cloth,' has red hair, allusions to which in the works of all our old dramatic writers are far too numerous to require specific reference.' There is, however, only *one* such reference in Shakespeare; in As You Like It, iii. 4. 9. See D. ii. 264, 265.

---

[1] In the Exeter Book, ed. Thorpe, p. 300. The poem begins :—Đūs frōd fæder frēo-bearn lærde.'

GLOSSARIAL INDEX

(For words beginning with þ, see after *T*; for words beginning with ȝ, see after *Y*.)

The following abbreviations are used in a particular sense:—*v.*, verb in the infinitive mood; *pr. s., pt. s.*, the *third* person singular of the present or past tense; *pr. pl., pt. pl.*, the *third* person plural of those tenses, except when 1 *p*. or 2 *p*. (first person or second person) is especially mentioned; *imp. s., imp. pl.*, the *second* person singular or plural of the imperative mood; *pp.*, past participle; *pres. part.*, present participle. Also *adj.*, adjective; *adv.*, adverb, &c., as usual. The A.S. (Anglo-Saxon) forms are usually added, as they best explain the forms. Other abbreviations are Icel., Icelandic; O.F., Old French; which are readily understood.

As in the Notes, the references are to Text B, unless 'a.' or 'c.' is expressly prefixed.

A, *for* On, in; A wold, in your power, at your disposal, 182. *See* Wold.

Abidist, 2 *pr. s.* abidest, 541.

Ac, but, 149, 163, 294. A.S. *ac.*

Acreis, *s. pl.* acres, 122.

A-drede, 2 *pr. pl. subj.* dread, a. 41. A.S. *ondrǣdan.*

Aferd, *pp.* afraid, frightened, 696. A.S. *āfǣred.*

After, *prep.* according to, 681; in imitation of, 297; for the help of, 699; Aftir þat, according as, 82.

Again, *prep.* against, 148. A.S. *ongēan.*

A-go, *pr. s. subj.* may depart, a. 220; Agoþ, *pr. s. as fut.* will depart, a. 221. A.S. *āgān.*

Ahte, *s.* property, wealth, 185, 250, 254, 522, 665. A.S. *āht.*

Ahte, *pt. s. subj.* were to possess, a. 121. A.S. *āgan*, pt. t. *āhte.*

Al, *adv.* altogether, 658; all, wholly, 83.

Al, *adj. as sb.* all, everything, 481; *pl.* Alle, all, 482, 612; *gen. pl.* Alre, of all; Ure alre, of us all, 96; Alre beste, best of all, most, 165.

Alfred (a. Ealured), Alfred, 9, &c.

Alfrich (a. Alurich), Ælfric, 7.

Alopeð, *pr. pl. as fut.* will loathe, will hold (thee) as odious, 671. *See Aloathe* in N.E.D.

Al-so, just as, 510.

Amendiþ, *pr. s.* amends, makes better, 709.

Amorȝe, on the morrow, 464.

A-nicht, in the night, 467.

Appel, *s.* apple, 306.

Areche, *v.* reach after, control, a. 454. A.S. *ārǣcan.*

Arede, 2 *pr. s. subj. as imp.*, receive as advice, accept, follow, a. 320. *See* Ared-tu. (This sense seems peculiar to this passage.)

Ared-tu (MS. B. Aretu), receive thou as advice, decide thou according to, 318. *See* Arede.

Aren, *pr. pl.* are, 582.

Areȝe (a. arewe), *adj. as sb.* cowardly one, bad-hearted man, 228, 236, 244, 245. A.S. *earg.*

Arixlye, *v.* rule, have the mastery, a. 453. See note.

Arme, *adj. pl.* poor, 39, 594. A.S. *earm.*

Armes, *s. pl.* arms, weapons, 649.

Armþe, *s.* poverty, 523. A.S. *iermþu.*

A-swunde, *pp.* vanished, a. 117. A.S. *āswindan.*

At-go, *pr. s. subj.* go from, depart from, leave, 220. See note.

At-hinden, *adv.* behind his back, 349. A.S. *æt-hindan.*

Atte, *for* At the, in the, 372; Atten ende, at the end, 570.

A-vynde, *v.* find out, find, a. 409. A.S. *onfindan.*

Awei, away, 508.

Awelde, *v.* control, a. 442. Cf. E. *wield.*

Ayhte, *s.* property, wealth, a. 185. *See* Ahte.

Aȝen, *prep.* against, 146. *See* Again.

A-ȝueþe, in youth, 149. *See* ȝueþe.

Baldure, *adj.* bolder, 639. (*Read* balder.)

Bale, *s.* bale, evil, grief, 397. A.S. *bealu.*

Bale-siþes, *s. pl.* times of adversity, 280. A.S. *bealu-sīð.*

Banne, *v.* curse, 443. A.S. *bannan.*

Barin (*for* Barn), *s.* bairn, child, 589; Baren, 625. A.S. *bearn. See* Bern.

Ben, *v.* be, 64, 639; Beon, *v.,* a. 104; Beð, *pr. s. as fut.* shall be, 321, 380: Beoþ, a. 114, 116; Ben, *pr. pl.* are, 75; Be, *pr. s. subj.* be, 65. A.S. *bēon.*

Benche, *dat.* a bench, seat, 626.

Berke, *pres. s. subj.* barks, 653, A.S. *beorcan.*

Bern, *s.* bairn, child, a. 430. *See* Barin.

Bes, *2 pr. s. as fut.* shalt be, 509; Best, art, 557. A.S. *bist.*

Best, *adv.* best, 621.

Bet, *adv.* better, 436, 604; Bett, 503. A.S. *bet.*

Bet, *imp. s.* beat, 623.

Beter, better, 447; Betere, 449, 490, 513.

Beuir, *adj.* trembling, 627. Cf. M.E. *beveren,* to tremble.

Bewen, *ger.* to bow, to bend, incline, 294. See *bēȝen* in Stratmann. *See* Buwe.

Bi, *prep,* by, according to, 249; beside, near, 667.

Bicche, *s.* bitch, 652.

Bi-cumen, *v.* become, come, a. 383; Bicome, *pt. s. subj.* would befit, 490, 513.

Bide, *imp. s.* beseech, pray, 602, 630; Bidde, 1 *pr. s.* 588, 625. A.S. *biddan,* imp. s. *bide.*

Bi-delid, *pp.* deprived, 558. A.S. *bedǣlan.*

Bi-fuliþ, *pr. s.* befouls, brings disgrace upon, 658. A.S. *befȳlan.*

Biforen, *prep.* before, 273; þe biforen, before thee, 628; *adv.* before thy face, 237; to his face, 348.

Biginne, *2 pr. s. subj. as imp.* begin, 415; Bi-gan, *pt. s.* began, 331*; Bi-gon, *pt. s.* began, did, a. 13. (Read *gon,* did.)

Bihait (a. bihat), *pr. s.* promises, 347. A.S. *behātan.*

Bi-hindin, *adv.* behind your back, 238.

Bihoue, *dat.* behoof, profit, a. 96. Cf. A.S. *behōflīc,* necessary.

Bihouith, *pr. s.* it behoves, 87. A.S. *behōfian.*

Bikechen (a. bikachen), *v.* ensnare, entrap, 359. Lit. be-catch. M.E. *bicachen.*

Bileuen, *v.* abide, survive, 586; Bileuið, *pr. pl.* 549. A.S. *belǣfan.*

Bilif, *s.* sustenance, 96. A.S. *bīleofa.*

Bilimpiþ, *pr. s.* happens, 486. A.S. *belimpan.*

Biluken, *v.* enclose, comprehend, 420; Biloken, *pp.* locked, shut, 554. A.S. *belūcan*; pp. *belocen*.

Bimenen, *v.* bemoan, lament, 194; Bimeniŏ, *pr. s. as fut.* will bemoan, 237. A.S. *bemǣnan*.

Binimiþ, *pr. s.* deprives (him) of, 539. A.S. *beniman*.

Binnen, *prep.* within, 527. A.S. *binnan, be-innan*.

Bi-schune þe, *imp. s.* shun, avoid (for thyself), a. 368. Lit. *be-shun*.

Biscopis, *pl.* bishops, 3.

Bi-sette, *v.* employ, put to good use, 674. Cf. Chaucer, C.T., Prol. 279.

Bisides, *prep.* beside, 575; Bisiden, 636.

Bismare-word, *s.* reproachful speech, reviling talk, 622. A.S. *bismer*, insult.

Biswiketh, *pr. s. as fut.* will deceive, will betray, 651; Biswike, *pp.* disappointed, a. 116. A.S. *beswīcan*, pp. *beswicen*.

Bit, *pr. s.* bites, 657; Bitiþ, 652.

Bi-þan, by that, thereby, 339, 706.

Biþenke, 1 *pr. pl. subj.* let (us) bethink ourselves, let (us) endeavour, 400. A.S. *biþencan*.

Bitideŏ, *pr. s.* happens, 540; Bitidiþ, 429.

Bitoʒen (a. bitowe), *pp.* employed, bestowed, 158. A.S. *betogen*, pp. of *betēon*.

Bitter, *adj.* bitter, 307.

Bituenen, *prep.* between, amongst, 485.

Biwilen, *v.* beguile, 328.

Bi-ʒete, 2 *pr. s. subj.* mayst acquire, dost obtain, 497. A.S. *begietan*.

Biʒete, *s.* acquired property, gains; *here*, a share in thy gains, gift, 498. A.S. *begĕat*; Napier, O.E. Glosses; Sweet, A.S. Dict.; *beget*, sb., N.E.D.

Blessedness, *s.* happiness, c. 50.

Blisse, *s.* bliss, happiness, 49, 428.

Bliþe, *adv.* happily, joyfully, 528.

Blithnesse, *s.* happiness, 50.

Blod, *s.* blood, 472.

Boke, *dat.* book, a. 66.

Bold, *adj.* bold, 411.

Bolt, *s.* cross-bow bolt, 421. A.S. *bolt*.

Bon, *s.* bone, 425.

Booc-lerede, *adj. pl.* (men) learned in books, 4; Booc-lerid (*read* booc-ilerid), 66.

Bord, *s.* board, table, 417. A.S. *bord*.

Bote, unless, 69, 129; Bute, 132; Bote-ʒif, unless, 65, 398.

Boþen, both, 512.

Brekiþ, *pr. s.* breaks, 425.

Briht, *adj.* bright, fair, 306*.

Bringen, *v.* bring, 251; Brouhte, *pt. s.* a. 266.

Buh þe from, bow thyself from, go from, move from, 629; Bus (*for* bues *or* buʒes), 2 *pr. s. as fut.* shalt bow, shalt turn (towards), go (towards), 621. See the note.

Bure, *dat.* bower, lady's chamber, 309. A.S. *būr*.

Burie, *s.* abode (*lit.* borough), 527. A.S. *byrig*, dat. of *burh*.

Bury, *dat.* town, abode, 251. (*Rather read* bure, 'to thy bower'; *see* l. 309.)

Bus; *see* Buh þe from.

Bute, but, 131; unless, 132. *See* Bote.

Buuen, *prep.* above, upon, a. 436. A.S. *bufan, be-ufan*.

Buwe, *ger.* to bend, to incline, a. 294. *See* Bewen.

By-come, *pr. pt. subj.* it would befit, a. 209. *See* Bi-cumen.

By-hinde, behind, in the lurch, a. 194. *See* Bi-hindin.

By-hud, *imp. s.* hide, a. 243. A.S. *behydan*.

By-wite, *pr. s. subj.* may be conscious of, a. 246. A.S. *be-witan,* to watch over.

Can, *pr. s.* knows, 232, 330. *See* Con.

Catt, *s.* cat, kitten, 296.

Charigeth, *pr. s.* returns, c. 85. (For *cheriȝeth*). *See* Cherrið.

Chepynge, *s.* market, a. 373. A.S. *cĕapung.*

Cherl, *s.* peasant, 92. A.S. *ceorl.*

Cherrið (cherricd, a. churreþ), *pr. s.* returns, 85. A.S. *cierran.*

Chesen, *v.* choose, 249, 342; Cheseð, *pr. s.* 257; Ches, *imp. s.* 645, 662. A.S. *cĕosan.*

Chiden, *ger.* to chide, quarrel, 412, 414. A.S. *cīdan.*

Child, *s.* child, 428. A.S. *cild.*

Chirche, *s.* church, a. 91; Chyreche, *for* Chyrche, a. 373.

Clerc (a. clerek, b. cleric), *s.* clerk, learned man, 19.

Cniht, *s.* knight, 78, 87; Cnihtes, *gen.* 97; *pl.* 6. A.S. *cniht.*

Cnowen, *v.* know, 341; *ger.* to know, 88. A.S. *cnāwan.*

Cocken, *v.* wrangle, swagger, fight, 688. *See* Cock, *v.* (1), *in* N.E.D.

Cocker, *s.* wrangler, fighter, 704.

Cold, *adj.* cold, i. e. evil, baneful, 336. See note.

Comið, *pr. s. as fut.* will come, 409.

Companie, *s.* company, 709.

Con, *pr. s.* knows, a. 232. *See* Can.

Costes, *pl.* habits, qualities, 252; ways, 535. Icel. *kostr.* *See* Custe.

Cot-lif, *s.* cot-life, life in a cottage, 259. Icel. *kotlīfi,* humble life.

Coueren, *v.* recover, protect, aid, 595. *See Cover* in N.E.D.

Criste, *dat.* Christ, 34; Crist, *acc.* 42.

Cumið, *pr. s.* comes, 534.

Cunne, 2 *pr. s.* canst, 559.

Cunnes, *gen.* of kind; None cunnes, of no kind, 560; Manyes cunnes, of many a kind, a. 413; Alle cunnes, of every kind, 384. (In the last instance, the MS. once had *cunnes,* but the *s* has been partly erased.)

Cunnie, *pr. s. subj.* may know (how), can, 69. (Better *cunne,* as in A.)

Custe, *s. pl. f.* virtues, a. 252. A.S. *cyst;* *pl. cysta.* *See* Costes.

Cuð, *adj.* well known, 357. (But a. forcuð, wicked, hostile.)

Cuþe, *v.* make known, tell, a. 358; Cuþeþ, *pr. s. as fut.* will make known, a. 253; Cuþe, *pr. s. subj.* may make known, may show, 253. (Last sentence imperfect and uncertain.)

Cwethen, *s. pl.* sayings, c. 35. Cf. A.S. *cwide.*

Dar, *pr. s.* dare, 655.

Daȝis, *gen.* day's, 566; Daȝes, *pl.* life-days, 546.

Ded, dead, 701.

Dedes, *pl.* deeds, 322; Dedin, *pl.* 77.

Delen, *v.* distribute, 544. A.S. *dǣlan.*

Demen, *v.* deem, judge, give as judgement, 79. A.S. *dēman.*

Dere, *adj.* dear, 589; *pl.* 213.

Derling, *s.* darling, 11. A.S. *dĕorling.*

Desi, *adj.* foolish, 479. A.S. *dysig.*

Desieth, *pr. s.* acts foolishly, plays the fool, 464; Desiende, *pres. pt.* playing the fool; *as adv.* foolishly, 466. A.S. *dysian.*

Deþ (deit; a. doþ), *pr. s.* doth, 126; (b. doþ), 406; Deð, 470;

Deþ, *pr. s. as fut.* will do, a. 443.
A.S. *deð.*

Deȝh, *pr. s.* avails, 506. A.S
dēah. See Duȝen.

Diche, *dat.* ditch, 700.

Dom, *s.* judgement, decision,
84; Domis, *gen.* of judgement, 177.
In l. 40, the sentence is incomplete.

Don (a. do), *v.* to do, 289, 330*,
655; Doþ, *pr. s.* makes, 536;
Done, *pp. pl.* done, gone, 582.

Dote, *s.* a dotard, a foolish
person, 422. From the verb.

Douhter, *dat.* daughter, 550.

Doweþes, *gen.* of might, or of
Hosts, a. 177. *See* Duȝeðe; and
see note.

Dredin, 2 *pr. pl. subj.* may
dread, 41.

Dreiȝe, *s.* tediousness, annoyance, 303. See *Dreigh* in the
N. E. D. (But it is better to read
treȝe, i.e. affliction, a word very
often found in company with *tene.*)

Dreri, *adj.* sorrowful, sad, 263.

Drihtin, *s.* the Lord, 42, 176,
203; Drihten, 517; Driȝten, 599.
A.S. *dryhten.*

Drinkin, *v.* drink, 461.

Driuin, *ger.* to drive, 95;
Driuen, be driven, 202.

Dure, *s.* door, 85. A.S. *duru.*

Duste, *dat.* dust, 202.

Duȝen, *pr. pl.* avail, last, 546.
A.S. *dugon. See* Deȝh.

Duȝeþe, *s.* riches, wealth, 544;
Duȝeðe, 516. A.S. *duguþ.*

Dwales, *s. pl.* fools, 414. Goth.
dwals, foolish.

Ealde, *s.* old age, a. 441, 455.
See Elde.

Echere, any (lit. each), a. 241.

Edie, *adj. pl.* rich, wealthy, 39.
A.S. *ēadig.*

Edinesse, *s.* happiness, 154.
(MS. hednesse.) A.S. *ēadignes.*

Ef, *conj.* if, 486.

Eft, *adv.* again, a. 244, 495.
A.S. *eft.*

Egleche, *adj. pl.* bold, valiant,
6. See note.

Eke (heke), *adv.* also, 9. A.S.
ēac.

Elde, *s.* old age, 153, 534, 542,
557; a. 104, 110, 112; full age,
441. A.S. *ieldo. See* Ealde.

Elde, *acc.* old man, 614.

Elden, *ger,* to grow old, 536.

Elder, *adj.* older, 641.

Eldere, *gen. pl.* of our elders,
of our parents, 185.

Ende, *s.* end, 174; At þen ende,
at the end, 408. A.S. *ende.*

Engelonde (enkelonde), England, 12, 17, 24. A.S. *Englalond.*

Englene, *gen. pl.* of the Angles,
of the English, 10, 11, 26. See
note to l. 12.

Eni, *adj.* any, 324.

Eorþe, *s.* earth, a. 262, 436.
A.S. *eorþe.*

Er, *adv.* ere, previously, 489,
510; *conj.* before, 252. A.S. *ǣr.*

Eren, *s. pl.* ears, 494. A.S.
ēare, pl. *ēaran.*

Erewe, bad man, 236. *See*
Areȝe.

Erl, *s.* earl, 7, 74; Erles (herles),
pl. 5. A.S. *eorl.*

Erliche, *adv.* early, soon, 331*.

Erre (a. vrre), *s.* anger, 205.
A.S. *ierre.*

Erþe, *s.* earth, 126. *See* Eorþe.

Eþeling, *s.* prince, noble, 74
A.S. *æþeling.*

Eu, *pron. acc.* you, a. 214. A.S.
ēow.

Euen, *s.* evening, 475.

Euenliche, *adv.* impartially,
79.

Eueriches, *gen.* of each, 84.

Eure, your, a. 28; 675. A.S.
ēower.

Eure, *adv.* for ever, 203.

Eyhte, *s.* property, a. 220. *See*
Ahte.

Fadir, *s.* father, 54; Fader, 591; Fader, *gen.* a father's, a. 428; Fadiris, *gen.* 428.

Faire, *adj.* fair; On faire, in a fair woman, 256.

Faire, *adv.* fairly, pleasantly, 347.

Faires, *s. pl.* (apparently) fair things, precious things, fine things, 520.

Falewiþ, *pr. s.* loses colour, 579. A.S. *fealwian.*

Faren, *v.* go, travel, 379; behave, 689; Te faren = faren þe, go, get away, escape, 648; Fare, *pr. s. subj.* may happen, turn out, 98. A.S. *faran.*

Faste, *adv.* fast, tightly, 521. A.S. *fæste.*

Fe, *s.* property, goods, 192, 511.

Felde, *dat.* field, 169.

Fele, *pl.* many, 3, 4, 418, 535, 638; many things, 420. A.S. *fela.* See Feole.

Fele, *adv.* much, a. 196.

Fele, I *pr. s.* feel, experience, 578.

Fen, *s.* mud, 698.

Fend, *s.* enemy, 488.

Feole, *adj.* much, a. 353. *See* Fele.

Fere (a. vere), *s.* companion, 675; To fere, for a companion, 223, 645, 662. A.S. *fêra.*

Feye, *adj. pl.* fated to die, a. 170. A.S. *fæge.*

Fikil, *adj.* fickle, 356. A.S. *ficol.*

Filsten, *v.* assist, 604. A.S. *fylstan.*

Finden, *v.* find, 552; Findith, *pr. s. as fut.* will find, 409.

Flesshe (MS. fles), *dat.* flesh, meat that is being salted, 470. A.S. *flæsc.*

Floweþ, *pr. s.* flows in, a. 146; is full (like the sea), a. 197.

Fokel, *adj. as s.* a false one, 257. Apparently an incorrect form; due to confusion of A.S. *ficol,* fickle, with M.E. *fôken,* fraudulent. See Stratmann (s.v. *fâken*).

Fokel, *adv.* deceitfully, 349.

Foken, *pr. pl.* act falsely, are deceitful, 485. (Better *foknen.*) Cf. A.S. *fâcne,* deceitful.

Folewiþ, *pr. s.* follows, 331.

Folk[e], *dat.* to thy people, 590; *gen.* Folkes, of the people, 53. A.S. *folc.*

Fomen, *s. pl.* foes, 274.

Fon, *s. pl.* foes, 191. Pl. of *fo.*

Fône, *ger.*; *on to fone,* to take (upon him), to undertake, a. 88. A.S. *fônne, ger.* to seize. *See* Foþ.

For, *prep.* in the place of, 591.

For soþe, for truth, as truth, 669.

Forbod, *s.* prohibition, 446. A.S. *forbod.*

Forcuð, *adj.* wicked, hostile, a. 357. A.S. *forcûþ.* See note.

Fordrunken, *pp.* being extremely drunk, 465. A.S. *fordruncen,* þp.

For-farin, *v.* fare amiss, suffer, 222. A.S. *forfaran. See* For-vare.

For-hele, *imp. s.* entirely conceal, 244. A.S. *forhelan.*

Forleseð, *pr. s.* loses utterly, 207. A.S. *forlēosan.*

For-leten, *v.* wholly give up, a. 190; abandon, a. 394. A.S. *forlætan.*

For-loren, *pp.* utterly lost, 511. A.S. *forloren,* pp. *See* Forleseð.

For-swunken, *pp.* worn out with toil, wearied with labour, 292. Cf. A.S. *swincan,* to toil.

Forteþ, *pr. pl.* (they) lead astray, mislead, a. 334. A.S. *fortēon.* See note.

Forþ, forwards, onwards, a. 230; onward, 618; Forð daȝes, latter part of the day, twilight, 696. See note.

Forþan, forthat reason, because, a. 339. A.S. *for þām*.

For-þi, therefore, 243, 422; on that account, 183. A.S. *for-þȳ*.

Forto, how to, 89.

For-vare, *v.* fare amiss, a. 222; For-vareþ, *pr. s.* destroys, a. 366. *See* Forfarin.

For-yemeþ, *pr. s.* neglects, a. 207. A.S. *forgieman*.

For-yeteþ, *pr. s.* forgets, a. 208; *pp.* For-ȝeten, forgotten, 555. A.S. *forgietan*, pp. *forgeten*.

Foster, *s.* offspring, 551. See N.E.D.

Foþ, *pr. s. as fut.* shall receive, a. 407. *See* Fóne.

Frakele, *adj.* evil, bad, worthless one, a. 257. See note to l. 256.

Frakele, *adj.* evilly, ill, a. 349.

Fre, *adj.* liberal, 498. A.S. *frēo*.

Fremannes, *gen.* free man's, a. 417.

Fremede, *adj. as s.* a stranger, 129. A.S. *fremede, fremþe*.

Frend, *s.* a friend, 130, 489; *dat.* to (thy) friend, 480; *pl.* Frend, 552; Freond, a. 38; Frend[e], *dat. pl.* to (thy) friends, 545. (*Read* frende *or* frenden.)

Frendschipe, *s.* friendship, 373.

Friþ, *s.* safety, 92. A.S. *friþ*.

Fro, *prep.* from, 221. Icel. *frā*.

Frouere, *s.* solace, comfort, 26, 54, 62. A.S. *frōfor*.

Froueren, *v.* comfort, solace, 594. A.S. *frōfrian*.

Frumþe, *s.* the beginning, a. 129 (so in MS.; but wrongly; see the note).

Ful, *adv.* very, 120.

Fule, *adj. pl.* foul, disgraceful, 687. A.S. *fūl*.

Funden, 1 *pr. pl.* go, depart, 553. A.S. *fundian*.

Furþ, *adv.* continually, a. 171. A.S. *forþ*.

Gabbe, *imp. s.* prate, a. 411 Icel. *gabba*.

Gadeling (a. gedeling), *s.* fellow, low companion, 312. A.S. *gædeling*.

Gentile, *adj.* gentle; *hence* Gentile man, a gentleman, 707. O.F. *gentil*.

Genteleri, *s.* gentlemanly conduct, 708.

Gile, *s.* guile, 664.

Gin, *imp. s.* begin; Gin þu leuen, do thou believe, 352; Gin þu delen, do thou distribute, 544; *ill spelt* Ginne, 594, 595, 596; Ginne, *pr. s. subj.* it may begin (to him), 624; Ginnið, *pr. s.* begins; Ginnið leren, doth teach, 402. A.S. *on-ginnan*.

Gled, *adj.* glad, a. 304; Glade, *pl.* 48. A.S. *glæd*.

Glede, *dat.* glowing coal; Bi þe glede, beside the hearth, a. 315. A.S. *glĕd*.

Glednesse, *s.* gladness, a. 48. A.S. *glædnes*.

Gleu (a. gleaw), *adj.* wise, sagacious, 47; wise, prudent, 362. A.S. *glĕaw*.

Gliden, *v.* glide, go easily, 618.

Gnyde, *v.* crumble, a. 201. A.S. *gnīdan*.

God, *adj.* good, 45, 324, 340, 372; Godne, *acc. m.* a. 75. A.S. *gŏd*.

God, *s.* property, 675.

Godelike, *adj.* goodly, showy, 313.

Godnesse, *s.* goodness, 46.

Gold, *s.* gold, 125; Golde, *dat.* 124.

Gon, *pt. s.* did (lit. began), 13. *See* Biginne.

Grene, *adj.* green, 3c6. A.S. *grēne*.

Grennen, *v.* grin, 688. A.S. *grennian*.

Gres, *s.* grass, 126. A.S. *græs, gærs*.

Grewe, *pt. s. subj.* were to grow, 125. A.S. *grēowe,* pt. s. subj. of *grōwan.*

Gripen, *v.* grasp, seize; Gripen to, seize upon, 192. A.S. *grīpan.*

Gryþ, *s.* security, 91. Icel. *grið.*

Gyle, *s.* guile, a. 328.

Habbe, *pr. s. subj.* may have, 91, 132, 346; Hauen, *v.* have, 304; possess, 614; Hauest, 2 *pr. s.* hast, 181; Hauist, 227, 235; Haueþ, *pr. s.* hath, 223; Hauith, *pr. s.* hath, 205, 329; Hauedest, 2 *pt. s.* haddest, 242, 276; Hadde, *pt. s. subj.* were to possess, 121; should have, 123.

He, she, 262, 277, 279, 283, 284, 289, 292. A.S. *hēo. See* Hie, Hue.

Helden, *v.* hold, keep, 351; possess, 620; Helden, *pp.* held in, unuttered, 491. *See* Holden. A.S. *healdan.*

Hem, themselves, 485; them, 13; Heom, them, a. 13. A.S. *heom, him.*

Hen, *acc.* him, 672. A.S. *hine.*

Henne, *adv.* hence, 173, 175, 553. A.S. *heonan.*

Heo, they, a. 116. A.S. *hēo, hīe.*

Heorte, *s.* heart, a. 243. A.S. *heorte. See* Herte.

Heo-self, herself, a. 426.

Her, *adv.* here, 59, 151, 541. A.S. *hēr.*

Her, *s.* hair, 579. A.S. *hǣr.*

Herde, *s.* shepherd, protector, 10. A.S. *hierde.*

Here, *s.* (invading) army, 90. A.S. *here.*

Heregong, *s.* the march of an invading army, 10. A.S. *heregang.*

Heren, *v.* hear, c. 14; 529.

Herivnge, *s.* harrying, plundering, a. 90. A.S. *hergung.*

Herte, *s.* heart, 243, 581. *See* Heorte.

Heuid, *s.* head, 366. A.S. *hēafod.*

Hi (b. we, a. hi), they, 15. A.S. *hīe.*

Hi, *acc. f.* her, a. 275. A.S. *hīe.*

Hie, she, 293. *See* He.

Him (i. e. wisdom), it, 223; himself, 537; Hine, *acc.* him, a. 59, a. 302. A.S. *hine,* acc. m.

Hire, *acc.* her, 250, 275.

Hire, *poss. pron.* her, 249, 252.

Hire-selue, herself, 283, 426.

Hit, *pron.* it, 98, 176. A.S. *hit.*

Hokede, *adj.* furnished with hooks, i.e. thievish, 365. A.S. *hōcede,* curved.

Hoker, *s.* scorn, derision, 670. A.S. *hōcor.*

Hokerful, *adj.* scornful, 670; Hokerfule, 663.

Holden, *v.* hold, keep, 72, 521; Holdin, *v.* possess, 154; Holde, 1 *pr. s.* account, a. 422. *See* Helden.

Honden, *s. pl.* hands, 365.

Hore, *adj.* as *s.* hoary-headed man, 627. A.S. *hār.*

Horeling, *s.* unchaste man, 704.

Horse, *dat.* horse, horseback, 313.

Howyen, *v.* take thought, be sad, a. 135. A.S. *hogian.*

Hu, how, 15, 71. A.S. *hū.*

Hue, she, 273, 321, 327, 330. *See* He.

Huge, *adj.* great, 697, 709.

Hunger, *s.* famine, a. 90.

Hunt-seuinti, seventy, 122. A.S. *hundseofontig.*

Hure (a. heore, b. ȝure), their, 15.

Hwanne, when, a. 173, 178; Hwenne, 178, a. 175; Hwen, 175.

Hwar-so, *adv.* wherever, 380.

Hwat, what, 131.

Hweder-so, whithersoever, 569. *See* Hwider-so.

Hwenne, when, 178; Hwen, 175. *See* Hwanne.

Hwider-so, *adv.* whithersoever, a. 380. *See* Hweder-so.

Hwile, *s.* while, time, 311*, 393. A.S. *hwīl.*

Hwilis, whilst, 224; Hwile, 407, 546.

Hwo, whoso, whosoever, 59, 223; (they) who, 219.

Hwoso, who-so, whosoever, 298.

Hwych-so, whatsoever, a. 82.

Hyne, *acc.* him (i. e. wisdom), it, a. 219, 223. *See* Hine, s.v. Him.

I, *prep.* in, 557.

I (MS. Hi), I, 339. *See* Ich.

I-auhteð, *pr. s.* reckons, calculates, estimates, a. 255. A.S. *ge-eahtian.*

Ibidest, 2 *pr. s.* dost obtain, dost possess, a. 430. A.S. *gebīdan,* to await, meet with.

Ibod, *s.* command, a. 445. A.S. *gebod.*

Iboren, *pp.* born, a. 448; Iborin, 210. A.S. *geboren,* pp.

Iburep, *pr. s.* it behoves, a. 75. A.S. *gebyrian.*

Ich, *pron.* I, 214, 576. A.S. *ic.*

Icheose, *v.* choose, a. 341; Icheoseþ, *pr. s.* a. 257. A.S. *gecēosan.*

Icouere, *v.* obtain, secure, a. 342. See note.

Icweme, *pr. s. subj.* may please, may satisfy, c. 68. (But doubtless an error for *icunne,* i. e. may know. In which case read *he* in l. 67.)

Idelnesse, *s.* idleness, a. 154.

Idilschipe, *s.* idleness, 286.

Idrowe, *pp.* endured, undergone, a. 157. A.S. *gedrogen,* pp. of *gedrēogan.*

I-dryue, *pp.* driven, a. 95. A.S. *gedrifen,* pp. of *drīfan.*

Ifon, *s. pl.* foes, a. 191. A.S. *gefān,* pl. of *gefā.*

Ifurn, *adv.* formerly, long ago, a. 335. A.S. *gefyrn.*

Ihasteð, *pr. s.* hastes, acts in haste, 255. O.F. *haster.*

Iherest, 2 *pr. s.* hearest, a. 355.

I-herin, *v.* hear, 14; Iheren, 495. A.S. *gehīeran.*

Ihid, *pp.* hidden, 522. A.S. *gehȳdd,* pp. of *(ge)hȳdan.*

Ihurd, *pp.* heard (to be), a. 300. *See* I-herin.

Ildre, *gen. pl.* of our elders, of our parents, a. 185. A.S. *ieldran,* pl. parents.

Ilef, *imp. s.* believe, a. 352; trust, a. 196. *See* Ileuen.

Ilered, *pp.* instructed, a. 66. A.S. *gelæred,* pp.

Ileste, *v.* last, endure, a. 225, a. 387. A.S. *gelæstan.*

Ileuen, *v.* believe, 690; Ilef, *imp. s.* believe, a. 352; trust, a. 196. A.S. *gelīefan.*

Iliche, *adv.* alike, equally, 376. A.S. *gelīce.*

Ille, *adv.* ill, badly, severely, 652, 657.

I-multen, *v.* melt, a. 385. A.S. *gemyltan.*

Inne, within, 555. A.S. *innan.*

Inoh, *adj.* enough, 523; Inowe, *pl.* sufficient, a. 199. A.S. *genōh,* pl. *genōge.*

Iqueme, *pr. s. subj.* may please, a. 156. A.S. *gecwēman.*

Is, *pron. acc. pl.* them, 123. See note.

Isaid, *pp.* said, 329.

Ischapen, *pp.* decreed, destined, a. 143. See note.

Iselþe, *s.* (*miswritten* his elþe), good fortune, a. 362. A.S. *gesælþ.*

Isene, *adj. pl.* apparent (as being), a. 115. See note. A.S. *gesīene.*

Iseye, 2 *pr. s. subj.* were to see, should see, a. 273. Cf. A.S. *gesēon.*

Ishoten, *pp.* shot, discharged, 421. A.S. *gescoten,* pp. of *scēotan.*

Isowen, *pp.* sown, a. 123. A.S. *gesāwen,* pp. of *(ge)sāwan.*

Istreon, *s.* acquisition, a. 185. A.S. *gestrēon.*

Iuel, *adj.* evil, 258; difficult, 294. A.S. *yfel.*

Iuele, *adv.* ill, 261. A.S. *yfele, yfle.*

I-vere, *s.* companion; To i-vere, as a companion, a. 219. *See* Fere.

I-vo, *s. pl.* foes, a. 274. *See* Ifon.

Iwinþ, *pr. s.* gains, a. 151. A.S. *gewinnan.*

Iwrapþed (a. iwreþþed), *pp.* incensed, 321; Iwreþþed, angered, a. 276. Cf. A.S. *gewrāðian,* to incense; *gewrāðan,* to be angry.

Iwriten, *s. pl.* writings, records, a. 103, 109. Cf. A.S. pl. *gewritu.*

Iwurche þe, *imp. s.* make for thyself, procure, a. 374. A.S. *gewyrcan.*

Iwurþe, *v.* become, be, a. 263, a. 299, a. 435; Iwurþen, become, turn, 397; Iwurþe, *pr. s. subj.* may be, may happen, 571; let be done, 572. A.S. *geweorþan.*

Kenliche, *adv.* keenly, fully, 88.

Kenne, *pr. s. subj.* may know, understands, 68. (*Read* i-kenne, *for the metre.*) Cf. A.S. *cennan,* Icel. *kenna.*

Keren, *v.* select, choose out, 665. See note. Cf. A.S. *cyre,* choice.

King, *s.* king, 12, 17; Kingis (kinhis), *pl.* 2.

Lage, *s.* law, c. 8, c. 97. A.S. *lagu.*

Lageliche, *adv.* lawfully, c. 72; *adj.* lawful, c. 77.

Lasse, less, 461. A.S. *lǣssa.*

Lasten, *v.* last, 387. A.S. *lǣstan.*

Lat, *imp. s.* let, 614; *pr. s.* lets, 98. *See* Leten.

Lawe, *dat.* law, 8. A.S. *lagu.* *See* Laȝe.

Laweliche, *adv.* lawfully, 72; Laueliche, 77.

Laȝe, *s.* law, rule, 97. *See* Lawe.

Lede, *dat.* people; In lede, among the people, 335; Leden, *pl.* 27, 612; Ledin, *pl.* 39. A.S. *lēod. See* Leode.

Leden, *v.* to lead, 519; *v.* guide (thyself), conduct (thy life), 559; *ger.* to govern, 76; Lede, *v.* lead, 16; control, a. 351. A.S. *lǣdan.*

Lef, *adj.* lief, dear, 213. (Read *leue,* pl.) *See* Leue.

Leme, *s.* lucid appearance, shininess, radiance, 306*. A.S. *lēoma,* radiance.

Lengen, *v.* prolong, 392. A.S. *lengan.*

Lengest, *adv.* longest, 351. A.S. *lengest.*

Leode, *dat.* people, a. 370; *pl.* a. 40, a. 212. *See* Lede.

Leof, *adj.* dear, a. 370; Leoue, *pl.* a. 38. A.S. *lēof. See* Lef.

Leorny, *v.* learn, a. 107; Learneþ, *pr. s.* a. 101. A.S. *leornian.*

Leoþ, *s.* song, a. 333. (MS. loþ.) A.S. *lēoþ.*

Leoue, *adj. pl.* dear, a. 38. A.S. *lēof. See* Leof.

Leren, *v.* teach, 214, 402; Lerin, *v.* 13; Leren, *v.* learn, 637; Lere, 1 *pr. s.* teach, 608; Leriþ, *pr. s.* teaches, 287; Lere, *imp. s.* 432, 640; Ler þu þe, *imp. s.* teach thou thyself, learn, 367. A.S. *lǣran.*

Les (a. lest), 2 *pr. s.* lettest, allowest, 437. *See* Leten; and cf. Bus.

Lese, *adj.* false, 663. A.S. *lēas.*

Lesen, *ger.* to lose, 366. A.S. *lēosan.*

Lesinge, *s.* leasing, lying, 363; Lesing, 671. A.S. *lēasung.*

Lest, *pr. s.* 2 p. lettest, permittest, a. 437. *See* Leten.

Lest, least, 650.

Lesten, *v.* last, endure, 225; Lestinde, *pres. pt.* enduring, 474. A.S. *lǣstan.*

Leten, *v.* abandon, cease, give up, 277; leave, 394, a. 194; Letin, *v.* resign, 166, 179, 190; Lete, *v.* give up, a. 277; Let, *pr. s.* lets, a. 453; Letet (*for* Let it), let it go, disregard it, 525; Let þe, behave thyself, 598. A.S. *lǣtan.*

Lepe-bei, *adj.* pliant, lissom, unstable, 692. See note.

Lepere, *adj. pl.* evil, bad, 287. *See* Luþere.

Letteris, *s. pl.* letters, writings, 69.

Leue, *s.* belief, trust, 548. A.S. (*ge*)*lēafa.*

Leue, *voc.* lief, dear, 574. *See* Lef.

Leuen, *v.* believe, 352; Leue, *imp. s.* trust, 196. A.S. *gelīefan.*

Leȝen, *v.* lie to, deceive, 163; *ger.* to deceive, 368. A.S. *lēogan.*

Libben, *v.* live, a. 203. A.S. *libban. See* Liue.

Liche, *s.* body, 471. A.S. *līc.*

Lif, *s.* life, 15, 44, 178.

Ligen (*sic*), *v.* lie, lie down, 467.

Liht[e], *dat.* light, 566.

Lihte, *adv.* lightly, easily, a. 290.

Likeþ, *pr. s.* it pleases, 525; Likiþ, pleases, 234, 481; Like, *pr. s. subj.* may like, likes, 137; Likin, 2 *pr. pl. subj.* may please, 43. A.S. *līcian.*

Listeliche, *adv.* artfully, slily, 666. A.S. *listelīce.*

Listis, *s. pl.* arts, 560; contrivances, 638. A.S. *list.*

Liþen, *v.* listen to, pay attention to, c. 27. Icel. *hlȳða.*

Litil, *adj.* small, 431.

Liue, *v.* live, 547; Liuin, 203; Livin, 203; Liuiȝende, 1 *pres. pt.* living, 278. *See* Libben.

Liue, *dat.* life, 565; Liuis, *gen.* 40, 162. (*Wenen* governs the genitive.)

Liȝen, *v.* lie, tell lies, 670. A.S. *lēogan.*

Loare, *dat.* lore, teaching, c. 66. (Spelman has *loage,* perhaps meaning 'law'.) A.S. *lār.*

Lokin, *v.* observe, regard, pay heed to, 70; Locen, *ger.* to take care, c. 98; Loke, *imp. s.* regard, 371; take heed, 499, 501; Loke, *pr. s. subj. as imp.* let him look (to it), 98. A.S. *lōcian.*

Lond, *s.* land, 71, 76; Londe, *dat.* the country, 379.

Lone, *s.* loan, gift, 186; *dat.* loan, gifts, 564. (The true form is *loon* or *lōn; lone* is a dat. form used as a nom.) Icel. *lān.*

Longe, *def. adj.* tall, 692; Long, 680; Longes, *gen.* (after *weneþ*), long, 162. *See* Liuis.

Lore, *s.* teaching, 708. A.S. *lār. See* Loare.

Lorþeu, *s.* instructor, teacher, a. 105. See note.

Loð, *adj.* hateful, 363; Loþe, *acc.* hostile one, enemy, a. 350; *pl.* hateful, suspected, 487. A.S. *lāð.*

Louerd, *s.* lord, master, 301, 563, 591; Louird, 28, 44, 177; *gen.* lord's, 685. A.S. *hlāford.*

Louien, *v.* love, 599; Lovin, 2 *pr. pl. subj.* may love, 43; Louede, *pt. s.* 20. A.S. *lufian. See* Luue.

Lude, *adv.* aloud; Lude and stille, aloud and in silence, i. e. under all circumstances, 325; a. 439. See note to l. 325.

Luden, *s. pl.* noises, noisy utterances, 687. Cf. A.S. *hlȳd;* see note.

Lufsum, *adj.* pleasing, loveable, 18. A.S. *lufsum.*

Lusninde, *pres. part.* listening, watchful, 646, 654. See note to l. 645.

Lustin, *v.* listen to, 28; Lust, *imp. s.* 212; Lvsteþ, *imp. pl.* a. 212. A.S. *hlystan.*

Lustlike, *adv.* eagerly, with pleasure, 212. A.S. *lustlīce.*

Lutel, *adj.* little, a. 431; Lutele, *dat.* 395. A.S. *lȳtel.*

Lutel, *adv.* for a little time, 387; Lutil, little, 194.

Luþere, *adj.* bad (man), 651, 654; evil-hearted, 646; *pl.* evil, 364. A.S. *lȳðre. See* Leþere.

Luue, *imp. s.* love, a. 371; Luuede, *pt. s. subj.* might love, might enjoy, a 165; Luviende, *pres. pt.* c. 41. *See* Louien.

Lyen, *s.* a reward, recompense, a. 407. See note.

Lyeþ, *pr. s.* deceives, a. 163.

Lyues, *gen.* (*after* weneþ), life, a. 162; Lyue, *dat.*; By þine lyue, in your life, a. 318. A.S. *līf.*

Madmes, *s. pl.* treasures, 193, 198, 384. A.S. *māþm, māþum.*

Maist, 2 *pr. s.* mayest, 241.

Maister, *s.* master, 52, 299. O.F. *maistre.*

Makede, *pt. s.* made, 568. A.S. *macode,* pt. s.

Mameliþ, *pr. s.* babbles, prates, 492. Imitative; cf. E. *mumble.*

Me, *indef. pron.* one, 641; a. 347, 350. A.S. *man.*

Medis, *s. pl.* meadows, 94. A.S. *mǣd.*

Melten, *v.* melt, 385.

Meneþ, *pr. s. as fut.* will lament, a. 237. A.S. *mǣnan.*

Metes, 2 *pr. s.* meetest, 615.

Michte, *pt. s.* might, 341.

Mid, *prep.* with, 124, 219, 322. A.S. *mid.*

Middelerd, *s.* earth, world, 389. A.S. *middaneard, middangeard.*

Miht (mist), 2 *pr. s.* mayest, 239 (A.S. *miht*); Mihtin (mistin), 2 *pt. pl.* might, 21.

Mildeliche, *adv.* mildly, a. 37.

Mildist, *adj.* mildest, 52.

Minde, *dat.* remembrance, 601.

Mine, *pl.* my, 215.

Mixe, *s.* muck, dung, a. 385. A.S. *meox.*

Miȝte, *s.* strength, 539; Miȝten, *pl.* powers, 597. A.S. *miht.*

Moche, *pl.* great, 199.

Mod, *s.* fit of anger (lit. mood), 323; mood, attitude of mind, 479; mood, mind, 356; Mode, *s. dat.* mood, mind, courage; (perhaps) stable conduct, 676. (Hardly for *niod,* 'need,' as an assonance seems to be intended.) A.S. *mōd.*

Moder, *s.* mother, 297. A.S. *mōdor.*

Mon, *s.* man, 23, 82, 134, 204, 365; Monnes, *gen.* man's, 84; Monnis, *gen.* 432; Alle monnes spechen, all a man's sayings, 353; Monne, *dat. pl.* to men, 357; Monne, *gen. pl.* of men, 51. A.S. *mann;* gen. pl. *manna;* dat. pl. *mannum.*

Moneȝen, *v.* mention, remind, 530. A.S. *manian.*

Monimon, many a man, 160.

Mon-þewes, *pl.* manly virtues, a. 432. A.S. *mann-þēaw.*

Mony, many a, 204; Monie, *pl.* many, 2, 199; Moni, 306, 308. A.S. *manig.*

Mor, more, 242.

Morȝe-sclep, *s.* morning sleep, 473. A.S. *morgen,* morning.

Mot, *pr. s.* may, 143; Mote, *pr. s. subj.* a. 225. A.S. *mōt.*

Mowe, 2 *pr. s.* mayest, 547. *See* Moȝe.

Mowen, *ger.* to mow, 94; Mowin, *v.* mow, 83. A.S. *māwan.*

Moȝe, 2 *pr. s.* canst, 561. *See* Muȝe.

Muchil, *adv.* long, 474; Mukil, much, 368. A.S. *mycel,* for *micel.*

Multeplien, *v.* multiply, 675.

Munye, 1 *pr. s.* admonish, remind, a. 37. A.S. *manian.*

Murþe, *s.* pleasure, 567. A.S. *myrgþ*.

Museð, *pr. s.* mouseth, catches mice, 296.

Muð, *s.* the mouth, 492; Muþ, *a.* 356; Muþe, *dat.* 530. A.S. *mūð*.

Muȝe, 1 *pr. pl.* may, 403; *pr. s. subj.* may, 153; (a. mvwe), *pr. s.* may, can, 170; Muȝen, 2 *pr. pl.* may, 14. Cf. A.S. *magon. See* Moȝe.

Myd alle, with all, i. e. wholly, *a.* 190. A.S. *mid ealle*.

Nabbe, *pr. s. subj.* may not have, has not, *a.* 426. A.S. *nabban*.

Narruliche, *adv.* narrowly, niggardly, 519.

Nat, not, in no respect, 57.

Nauið, (*for* Ne hauið), hath not, 426 (MS. Trin. has *nauið*).

Ne, not, 127.

Nede, *s.* time of need, 372; Neden, *pl.* needs, 504. A.S. *nēod. See* Neode.

Nefere, never, 134.

Nei, *adv.* nigh, 582, 683.

Nele, *pr. s.* will not, *a.* 358. Cf. A.S. *nyllan*.

Nenne, *pl.* no, *a.* 414.

Neode, *s.* need, *a.* 213; *dat.* time of need, *a.* 316. *See* Nede.

Nere (*for* Ne were), would not be, *a.* 127; were not, 210; *a.* 448.

Neuedest (*for* Ne heuedest), hadst not, 514.

Neuer-mo, nevermore, *a.* 221.

Nexte, *adj.* next, nighest; *as s.* nearest neighbour or relative, 371.

Nim, *pr. s.* take, 673. A.S. *niman*.

Nis (*for* ne is), there is not, 168, 185.

Non, none, 426; None, no one, 551; Nones, *gen.* of no, 417. A.S. *nān*.

Not, *pr. s.* knows not, *a.* 172. A.S. *nāt*.

No-þing, nothing, naught, 58.

Nowiht, not at all, in no way, 284; Nouht, in no degree, 128; Nouht, *s.* nothing, 201.

Nu, *adv.* now, 575. A.S. *nū*.

Nule, *pr. s.* will not, *a.* 106, *a.* 295. Cf. A.S. *nyllan*.

Ny-wurþe (*for* Ne y-wurþe), *imp. s.* become not, *a.* 184. A.S. *weorðan*, to become.

O (*for* On), in, 610.

O, a, 121; one, a, *a.* 388.

O, *prep.* of, 373. (But probably short for *on*, i. e. in.)

O, *prep.* (for *on*), in, *c.* 66.

Of, *prep.* concerning, 280; from, 90, 637; out of, *a.* 129; for, 564.

Ofer-howeþ, *pr. s. as fut.* will disregard, despise, *a.* 445. A.S. *oferhogian*.

Of-reden, *v.* surpass in counsel, outwit, 642. See note.

Of-riden, *v.* outride, surpass in riding quickly, 641.

Ofte, *adv.* often, 484; Ofter, *comp.* more often, 324.

Of-þinkeþ, *pr. s.* it repents (him), he is grieved, 531. A.S. *of þyncan*.

Ogen, *adj.* own, *c.* 85. A.S. *āgen. See* Oȝene.

Oliue (*for* On life), in life alive, 260.

On, *prep.* in, 24 (see note), 151; *a.* 106.

On, *pr. s. as fut.* will grant, allow, will be in favour (of your misfortune), 240; will allow, *a.* 242. A.S. *ann*, pres. t. of *unnan*.

On and tuenti, one and twenty, 668.

Onder, *prep.* under, 64.

One, *adj.* alone, 509; *dat.* 243.

One, *adv.* alone, only, 45, 49, 51, 53, 176; by himself, *a.* 70. A.S. *āna*.

One (*for* On a), in a, 395.

One, *error for* On, *prep.* in, 632.

Onsuerren, *v.* answer, make answer, 666.

Ore, *s.* favour, mercy, a. 241. A.S. *ār*.

Orgul-prude, *s.* great pride, arrogance, 286. O.F. *orgoil*, *orguil*, pride.

Oþer, or, 616.

Oþere, *pl.* others, 342; Oþir, *s.* other, 585; Non oþir, not otherwise, 330.*

Oþer-hwile, *adv.* sometimes, 327.

Ou, you, a. 29.

Ouer, *prep.* above, 600; Ouir, over, of, 44.

Ouer-gangin, *v.* transgress, 446. A.S. *ofergangan*.

Ouer-goð, *pr. s.* surpasses, 217. A.S. *ofergān*.

Ouer-prute, *s.* excessive pride, a. 286. Cf. A.S. *ofer-prūt*, arrogant.

Over, *prep.* beyond, apart from, a. 342.

Owene, own, 440; Owe, a. 224; Owere, *dat. f.* a. 85. A.S. *āgen*. *See* Oȝene.

Ower, yours, a. 213.

Oȝene, *adj.* own, 85, 167; Oȝe, 85. A.S. *āgen*.

Plouis, *s. pl.* ploughs, 95.

Pouere, *adj. pl.* poor, 375; Poure, a. 39. O.F. *povre*.

Prude, *adj. pl.* proud, 5; Prute, a. 5. A.S. *prūt*.

Pruden, *v.* be proud of, boast (himself), 686.

Quad, (a. queþ), quoth, said, 25, 61, &c. A.S. *cwaþ*.

Qued, *s.* a bad man, 702; aversion, scorn, a. 305. *See cwēd* in Stratmann, *quad* in Chaucer.

Quele, *pr. s. subj.* die, a. 156. A.S. *cwelan*.

Quemen, *v.* please, 691. A.S. *cwēman*.

Quene, *gen. s.* of a woman; (*or*) *gen. pl.* of women, 336. A.S. *cwene*, gen. pl. *cwena*, for *cwenena*.

Red, *s.* advice, counsel, 331, 336, 681; a. 330; 'for he desires evil counsel for thee,' 703. (Or read *rede*, v.; 'for he will counsel thee thine evil.') A.S. *rǣd*.

Rede, *def. adj.* red, red-haired, 702; Red, 680; Rede, red, *dat.* 124. A.S. *rēad*.

Reden, *v.* advise, 503; read, a. 103; Rede, a. 109; *pr. s. subj.* 602. A.S. *rǣdan*.

Rei, *adj.* fierce, angry, passionate, 682, 693. A.S. *hrēoh*.

Reid, *s.* counsel, 330; Reides, *pl.* 640. *See* Red.

Reme, *v.* to make room, to leave clear; þu ȝef him þe wei reme = do thou permit him to clear the way, 617; see the note. A.S. *rȳman*, O.Fries. *rēma*.

Reowe, *v.* rue, grieve, a. 456. A.S. *hrēowan*. *See* Rewen.

Rere, *v.* raise, procure, 302. A.S. *rǣran*.

Rewen, *v.* rue, grieve, 442; Rewe, be grievous to, a. 111. *See* Reowe.

Riche, *adj.* rich, 56; *pl.* rich people, 375.

Rid, þe, *imp. s.* ride thee, i. e. ride on, 230.

Riht, *s.* right, justice, 79. A.S. *riht*.

Rihtwis (riste-wis), *adj.* righteous, 55. A.S. *rihtwīs*.

Rimen, *v.* depart, lit. make room, 'clear out,' 173. *See* Reme.

Riȝten, *v.* right, set right, 596. A.S. *rihtan*.

Rowen, *ger.* to row, 145.

Ryhtwis, *adj.* righteous, a. 63. *See* Rihtwis.

Sadilbowe, *s.* saddle-bow, the upper front part of a saddle, 229. (Because it cannot hear what is said.)

Saiȝe, 1 *pr. s.* say, 339, 524; Saith, *prs. s. as fut.* will say, 231; Saiȝe, 2 *prs. s. subj.* (thou mayst) say, 480; Sai (*read* Saiȝe), 271.

Salomon, Solomon, 329, 405.

Salt, *s.* salt, 470.

Samne (n. Somnen), *v.* join, unite, 34. A.S. *samnian.*

Saulle, *s.* soul, 207; *pl.* souls, 33.

Sawe, *s.* saw, proverb, a. 361; Saȝe, 361; Sawen, *pl.* sayings, 35. A.S. *sagu.*

Saȝin, *v.* say, 631. *See* Saiȝe.

Scarneð, *pr. s. as fut.* will deride, 238. O.F. *escarnir, escharnir,* to deride; from O.H.G. *scern,* derision.

Schendful, *adj.* shameful, vile, a. 311. A.S. *scendan,* vb.; from *scand,* sb. disgrace.

Schene, *adj.* beautiful, 310. A.S. *scīene,* lit. 'showy.'

Schete, *s.* sheet, 310.

Scholde, *pt. s.* ought, 289.

Schondes, *gen.* of disgrace, 310. A.S. *scand.*

Schotte, *imp. s.* pay scot; hence, participate with, take part with, consort with, a. 411. A.S. *ge-scot,* contribution, payment.

Schullen, *pr. pl.* will surely, will be sure to, 191; 1 *pr. pl.* must, 179.

Sclepen, *v.* sleep, 468.

Scold, *s.* scold, scolding person, 412; Scolde, 705.

Scumes, *s. pl.* shades of twilight (?), a. 334. See note.

Sedis, *s. pl.* seeds, 93.

See, *s.* sea, a. 146, a. 197.

Se-flod, *s.* flood of the sea, flood-tide, 146, 197.

Segge, *v.* say, a. 239; 1 *pr. s.* a. 339; Seiȝe, 1 *pr. s.* say, 706;

Seiȝen, *v.* 576; Seien, *v.* tell, 239; Seieth, *pr. s.* says, speaks, 348; Segge, 2 *pr. s. subj.* thou say, a. 271; Sei, *imp. s.* 570. A.S. *secgan. See* Sey.

Selden, *adv.* seldom, 304; Selde, 693. A.S. *seldan.*

Sele, *s. dat.* happiness, 305. A.S. *sǣl.*

Seli, *adj.* happy, 378. A.S. (ge-)*sǣlig.*

Selliche, *adv.* wonderfully, 304. A.S. *sellīce.*

Selþe, *s.* good fortune, 362. A.S. *sǣlþ.*

Seluen, *acc. or dat.* himself, 64.

Senden, *pr. pl.* are, 219. A.S. *sindon.*

Sendeþ, *pr. s.* sends, 517.

Seorewe, *s.* sorrow, a. 332; Seruȝe, 332. A.S. *sorg.*

Sete, *s.* seat, 629.

Seð, *pr. s.* sees, 236.

Setin, *pt. pl.* sat, 2.

Seuorde, *dat.* Seaford, a. 1.

Sey, *imp. s.* say, tell, 229. *See* Segge.

Seȝe, *pt. pl. subj.* should see, 273.

Shal, shalt, must, 248; Shaltu, shalt thou, 358.

Shapen, *v.* happen, fall out, 143.

Shule, *pr. s. subj.* ought to, 71; Shulen, 1 *pr. pl.* shall, 552; Shullen, 1 *pr. pl.* must, 188; Scholde, *pt. s.* ought, 493; Shuldin, *pt. pl.* should, 16.

Sibbie, *adj. pl.* related (by blood), 484. A.S. *sibb,* relationship; *gesibb,* related.

Siforde, *dat.* Seaford, 1.

Siker, *adv.* securely, 218; certainly, 524. A.S. *sicor,* from L. *securus.*

Sikerliche, *adv.* safely, securely, 377.

Singen, *v.* sing, utter, 355; Singende, *pt. pres.* singing, 230.

Siþen, *adv.* afterwards, 623, 635. A.S. *siððan.*

Sitte, *v.* sit, dwell, a. 218; Sitten, *v.* remain, 378; Site, *imp. s.* sit thou, 575, 635. A.S. *sittan.*

Sixst, 2 *pr. s.* seest, 627.

Slit, *pr. s.* slides, slips, 700.

Smerten, *v.* to smart, feel pain, 624; Smerteþ, *pr. s.* pains, 695; Smeorte, *pr. s. subj.* may pain, a. 244. A.S. *smeortan.*

So, so, 350; as, 126, 470, 608.

Sone, *adv.* soon; *wel sone,* very soon, a. 253; quickly, 630, 632; soon, 421. A.S. *sōna.*

Sone, *dat.* son, 550; *voc.* 574. A.S. *sunu.*

Sor, *s.* sore, affliction, 241. A.S. *sār.*

Sore, *adv.* sorely, severely, a. 411, a. 456; 442.

Soreȝe, *s.* sorrow, grief, 235, 469; Sorw, 190. A.S. *sorg.*

Sory-mod, *adj.* sad, sad in mind, a. 446.

Sot, *s.* foolish man, 622; Sottis, *gen.* a fool's, 421; Sotte, *dat.* sot, fool, a. 412. A.S. *sot.*

Soþe, *adj. pl.* true, 577. A.S. *sōþ.*

Sowin, *ger.* to sow, 93; Sowith, *pr. s.* sows, 82; Sowen, *pp.* sown, 123. A.S. *sāwan.*

Spareþ, *pr. s.* spares, a. 451. A.S. *sparian.*

Speche, *dat.* speech, c. 22; Spechen, *pl.* 353.

Stable, *adj.* steadfast, 673.

Stelin, *v.* steal, 665. A.S. *stelan.*

Steorne, *adv.* sternly, cruelly, a. 302. A.S. *styrne.*

Steren, *v.* (lit. steer), rule, provide for, 562. A.S. *stīeran.*

Sticke, *dat.* stick, 697.

Stille, *adj.* silent, 424, 656; *adv.* in silence, noiselessly, 325, 653.

Ston (*for* stone), *dat.* stone, 697.

Stonden, *v.* stand, 628.

Stondes, *gen.* hour's, 311.* A.S. *stund.* *See* Stunde.

Stoni, *adj.* stony, hard, 694.

Stren (a. istreon), *s.* acquisition, 185. A.S. *strēon, gestrēon.*

Strenȝþ, *s.* strength, 561.

Stretes, *s. pl.* streets, 616.

Stronge, *adj.* difficult, 145; Strong, strong, 18.

Stunde, *dat.* hour, time, 395. *See* Stondes.

Suich, such, 83.

Suiþe, *adv.* very, 8.

Sukeþ (MS. *has* súȝh *in l.* 469, suket *in l.* 471), sucketh, *or rather* soaketh, 469, 471. A.S. *sūcan,* to suck; *socian,* to soak.

Swich, such, 239, 526. (Perhaps in l. 239 read *swiche; but see l.* 241.)

Swift, *adj.* quick, 282.

Swikelne, *adj. acc. m.* deceitful, a. 356. A.S. *swicol.*

[**Swinker,** *s.* toiler, 150.]

Swinkin, *ger.* to toil, labour, 147; Swinkeþ, *pr. s.* toils, labours, a. 150. A.S. *swincan.*

Swiþe, *adv.* greatly, 18; very, extremely, 157; excessively, a. 135; decidedly, 318; To swiþe, too much, 196. A.S. *swīðe,* adv.

Swo, *adv.* so, 56, 269, 312, 405; as, 293. A.S. *swā.*

Swóte, *s. dat.* sweat; A swote, in sweat, with sweat, a. 292. A.S. *swāt.*

Swoti, *adj.* covered with perspiration, 292. A.S. *swātig.*

Tales, *s. pl.* tales, 413.

Taȝte, *pt. s.* taught, 444, 634. A.S. *tāhte,* pt. t. of *tǣcan.*

Te (*for* The, *after* And), the, 236; c. 82, 91, 92.

Te (*for* þe, *after* it), *dat.* to thee, 524.

Teleþ, *pr. s. as fut.* will blame, a. 238. A.S. *tǣlan.*

Tellen, *ger.* to tell, report, 416; **Telle,** 1 *pr. s.* account, 422; **Tellit** (*for* Telle it), tell it, 669.

Ten, *v.* show, display (himself), 685. A.S. *tēon.*

Tene, *s.* grief, sorrow, 303. A.S. *tēona.*

Ti (*for* Thi, *after* þat), thy, 232.

Tidinges, *s. pl.* tidings, 416.

To, *prep.* to; Him to, into him, 469.

To, too, 184, 282.

To-delen, *v.* separate, 583. A.S. *todǣlan.*

To-moreuin (*for* To-morwen), to-morrow, 508.

To-teone, *v.* vex greatly, a. 303. *See* Tene.

To-trayen, *v.* torment, vex extremely, a. 303. Cf. A.S. *trega,* grief, affliction.

Treowe, *adj.* true, straight, a. 295; *miswritten* Ter, 295. A.S. *getrēowe,* adj.

Tresten, *v.* trust, rely, 505.

Trowe, *pr. s. subj.* may trust to, trusts to, 165. A.S. *trūwian.*

Trowþe, *s.* truth, 506. A.S. *trēowþ.*

Tune, *dat.* man's abode (lit. town), 534. See the note.

Tunge, *s.* tongue, 282, 425. A.S. *tunge.*

Turne, *v.* turn away, depart, a. 173.

Þan, *dat. m.* the, a. 87; *acc. m.* 614; **þane,** *acc. m.* a. 350, a. 352. A.S. *þām,* dat. ; *þone,* acc.

Þanen, thence, 151. A.S. *þanon.*

Þanke, *imp. s.* thank, 563. A.S. *þancian.*

Þanne, then, 191, 511, 563; when, 140, 164, 492, 650. A.S. *þanne, þonne,* then, when.

Þanne (*read* þan, *as in* a.), than, 324.

Þar, where, a. 347, a. 407. A.S. *þǣr.*

Þare, *dat. f.* the, a. 8, a. 316. A.S. *þǣre. See* þer.

Þarf, *pr. s.* need, ought, 161, 345, 461. A.S. *þearf.*

Þar-myde, therewith, thereby, a. 392.

Þar-of, therefrom, a. 188.

Þas, on that account, 436. A.S. *þæs.*

Þas, *acc. pl.* those, a. 170. A.S. *þās,* originally pl. of *þes,* this.

Þat, that which, 571.

Þaugh, though, 121; þau[h], 653. *See* þoh.

Þe, *rel. pron.* that, which, a. 36; 475; who, a. 219; þe þat, he that, a. 106; þe mon þe, the man who, a. 100. A.S. *þe.*

Þe, *dat.* to thee, 234, 481.

Þef, *s.* thief, 704.

Þeine, 2 *pr. s. subj.* serve, 499. A.S. *þēnian, þegnian.*

Þen, *acc. masc.* the, 365, 627, 646; cf. 174. *See* þan.

Þen, *adv.* when, 532. *See* þanne.

Þenchen, *ger.* to think, design, 288. A.S. *þencan.*

Þene, *acc. m.* the, a. 172, 174; that, a. 290. *See* þan.

Þenes, *s. pl.* thanes, 215. A.S. *þegn, þēn.*

Þenkeþ, *pr. s.* thinks, resolves, intends, 60; thinks, 246; þenkeð, 532; þenk, *imp. s.* 518. *See* þenchen.

Þenne, than, 450, 642; then, 166; þenne . . . þenne, then . . . when, a. 112, 114. *See* þanne.

Þeode, *dat.* people, nation, a. 369. A.S. *þēod.*

Þeoh, though, 138.

Þer, *adv.* where, wherein, 347.

Þer, *dat. fem.* the, 126. *See* þare.

Þer-after, *adv.* accordingly, c. 83.

þer-fro, from it, 188.

þer-inne, therein, 391.

þer-mide, therewith, 623. (*Two lines seem to have been lost before l. 623.*)

þer-to, to it, i. e. to come to it, 630.

þes, *gen. s.* of the, 97. A.S. *þæs.*

þe-seluen, *acc.* thyself, 562; *nom.* 547.

þet, that, 170. A.S. *þæt.*

þewes, *s. pl.* habits, manners, 287; virtues, 577; þewis, 432; þeues, 638; þeuues, good services, 500. A.S. *þēaw.*

þewiþ, *pr. s.* shouts, cries out, 699. (*Perhaps for* þeutiþ.) Cf. A.S. *þēotan*, to howl.

þey, though, a. 121.

þeynes, *s. pl.* thanes, a. 2. *See* þenes.

þin (*for* þen), *dat. of def. art.* to the, 228; *dat. or acc.* 244; *acc.* 245.

þinc, *imp. s.* suppose, 183. *See* þenchen.

þing, *s.* thing, personage, 18; þinge, *dat. pl.* things, 600.

þire, *dat. f.* thy, a. 243. A.S. *þinre*, dat. f. of *þin.*

þo, they, 75; them, those, 548. A.S. *þā*, pl. of *se.*

þoh, nevertheless, 294, 310, 483; þoch, though, 136, 220. A.S. *þēah.*

þohte, *pt. s.* thought, expected, 293.

þonkes, *s. pl.* thoughts, 482. A.S. *þanc, þonc*, thought.

þurh, *prep.* by means of, 361. A.S. *þurh.*

Uexynde, *pres. pt.* growing, a. 168. *See* Wexynde.

Unc, *dual*, us two, 583. A.S. *unc.*

Unselþe, *s.* misfortune, 148. *See* Selþe.

Unwurþ, *adj.* worthless, 316.

Up, *prep.* upon, 197.

Up-breidin, *v.* upbraid, 279.

Uppe, *prep.* upon, a. 197.

Ure, *gen. pl.* of us, 96; *poss. pron.* our, 178. A.S. *ūre.*

Ute, *adv.* outside, 554. A.S. *ūte.*

Uuele (=uvele), *s. dat.* evil, 135. *See* Yuil.

Vale, *adj* many, a. 418. *See* Fele.

Vayre, *adv.* fairly, a. 347, 348.

Velde, *dat.* field, a. 169. A.S. *feld.*

Veoh, *s.* property, a. 192 (MS. vouh.) A.S. *feoh.*

Vere, *s.* companion; To vere, as a companion, a. 223. *See* Fere.

Vnbeten, *pp.* not beaten, 450.

Vnboren, *pp.* unborn, 449.

Vnbuhsum, *adj.* disobedient, a. 450. Cf. E. *buxom.*

Vndrunkin, *pp.* not drunken, 459.

Vnfoldiþ (*for* umfoldiþ), *pr. s.* folds around, embraces, 659. Cf. A.S. *ymbclyppan*, to embrace.

Vnhelþe, *s.* lack of health, illness, a. 113.

Vnkeþe, *adj. pl.* strange, 535. A.S. *uncūð.*

Vnlede, *adj.* miserable, a. 337. A.S. *unlǣd*, poor.

Vnluden, *s. pl.* unpleasant noises, bad language, 689. See note.

Vn-meke, *adj.* impatient, 538.

Vnþeu, *s.* evil habit, ill habit, vice, a. 290; Vnþewes, *pl.* a. 368. A.S. *unðēaw.*

Vnwurð, *adj.* worthless, 120, 364.

Vnylimpe, *s.* misfortune, a. 148. A.S. *ungelimp.*

Vnyqueme, *adj.* displeasing, a. 444. A.S. *ungecwēme.*

Vordrye, *ger.* to further, a. 326. A.S. *fyrþrian.*

Vp-helden, *v.* uphold, sustain, 171. *See* Helden.

Vppon, *prep.* upon, a. 262. (MS. vppen.)

Vrre, *s.* anger, a. 205. A.S. *ierre, yrre.*

Vs-sulue, ourselves, a. 400*.

Vuel, *adj.* evil, worthless, a. 316; **Vuelne,** *acc. m.* evil, a. 330. A.S. *yfel. See* Yuil.

Vuele, *s. dat.* evil, a. 141.

Vurþere (a. furþer), *adj.* further, forwarder, greater, 128.

Vyches cunnes, of each kind, of every kind, a. 384. *See* Cunnes.

Wan, *adj.* wan, pallid, 580. A.S. *wann.*

Wane, *adj.* lacking, c. 57. *See* Wone.

War, *adj.* wary, prudent, 22. A.S. *wær.*

Weiȝe, *dat.* way, highway, 315; Weie (*better* wei), *acc.* 617; Weis, *pl.* 616. A.S. *weg.*

Wel, *adv.* well, 137, 143, 158; very, 18, 538; a. 120. A.S. *wel.*

Welden, *v.* possess, 193; enjoy, 526; control, 284, 537; govern, 440; **Weldin,** *v.* wield, acquire, 32; **Weldest,** 2 *pr. s.* possessest, a. 182; 388, 430, 543; Welde, *pr. s. subj.* may wield, possess, control, 138. A.S. *wealdan.*

Wele, *pr. s.* will, 529; *pr. s. subj.* may wish, will, 140; **Wille,** *pr. s.* will, 631. A.S. *wile. See* Wile, Welle.

Wele, *s.* weal, wealth, riches, 120, 127; prosperity, 142. A.S. *wela.*

Welle, *pr. s.* will, 631. *See* Wele.

Welþe, *s.* wealth, riches, 152, 181, 350, 382, 390; **Welþes,** *gen.* 558.

Wenden, *v.* go, depart, 175, 188; go, 584; come, 528; **Wende,** *v.* turn, apply himself, 434; Wen-

des, 2 *pr. s.* goest, 569; Went, *pr. s.* goes, 221. A.S. *wendan.*

Wene, *s. pl.* expectations, a. 114. A.S. *wēn.*

Wene, *v.* suppose, a. 231; **Wenen,** *v.* expect, 161, 345, 403; **Wenest,** 2 *pr. s.* expectest, 650; **Wenith,** *pr. s.* expects, 160, 344. A.S. *wēnan.*

Wenliche, *adj.* excellent, a. 105. A.S. *wēnlīc (woenlīc).*

Weole, *s.* wealth, a. 155. *See* Wele.

Wepen, *v.* weep, a. 267.

Werc, *s.* work, 20; **Werke,** *dat.* 22. A.S. *weorc.*

Werchin, *v.* work, do, 156; **Wercheþ,** *pr. s.* acts, 466. A.S. *wyrcan.*

Werd, *s.* troop, band (of men), 697. A.S. *werod.*

Were, 2 *pr. s.* wast, 510; *pt. s. subj.* would be, should be, 127, 292.

Weriin (a. werie), *ger.* to guard, protect, 89. A.S. *werian.*

Werlde, *dat.* the world, 31, 151, 182, 585; **Werldes,** *gen.* 382. A.S. *weorold.*

Werse, 475. *Read* Wo-so (*for* Hwo-so), whosoever.

Wexynde, *pres. pt.* growing up, a. 433; **Wexende,** a. 438. A.S. *weaxan.*

Widewis, *gen.* the widow's, 593.

Wif, *s.* wife, 248, 258.

Wiht, *s.* wight, person, 443. A.S. *wiht.*

Wike, *s.* office, employment, 316. A.S. *wice.*

Wile, 1 *pr. s.* will, 576. *See* Wele.

Wilis, *s. pl.* wiles, wily acts, 649.

Wille, *s.* will, wish, 58, 187, 380, 572; desire, 326; Wille to Criste, what is pleasing to Christ, 399. A.S. *willa.*

Wille, 1 *pr. s.* will, 214. *See* Wile.

Wimmon, *s.* a woman, 281,

308, 323. A.S. *wīfmann, wīmmann.*

Winnen, *ger.* to win, get, 152.

Wis, *adj.* wise, 8, 21, 132, 134, 406, 462 ; Wise, *pl.* 35. A.S. *wīs.*

Wisdome, *dat.* wisdom, 119. (In the Trin. MS. wisdō, *with the* e *cut away.*)

Wise, *s.* state, condition, 136, 232, 233 ; wise, way, manner, 400*. A.S. *wīse.*

Wisiste, wisest, 23.

Wisliche, *adj. pl. either* (1) certain, sure, 30 ; *or* (2) wise, prudent. (A. *has* wisliche, *adv.* certainly.) A.S. *wislīc,* adj. certain.

Wissin, *v.* teach, instruct, 29 A.S. *wissian.*

Wite, *s.* wise man, 633. A.S. *wita.* (MS. wid !)

Wite, *v.* know, a. 245 ; Wiste, *pt. s.* knew, 489 ; Wiste he, if he knew, a. 266. A.S. *witan.*

Witerliche, *adv.* verily, for a certainty, 701. Icel. *vitrliga.*

Wiþ, *prep.* against, a. 90 ; Wið, rom, 244 ; towards, 375, 592 ; by means of, 649.

Wið-alle, withal, 462.

Wið-innen, inside, 307 ; inwardly, 657. A.S. *wiþinnan.*

Wið-uten, *adv.* externally, 306 ; outwardly, 656 ; *prep.* without, 119. A.S. *wiþūtan.*

Witin, *v.* know, 245. *See* Wite.

Wiue, *dat.* wife, 319.

Wiueð, *pr. s.* wiveth, marries, 261. A.S. *wīfian.*

Wlanc, *adj.* proud, fine, 315 ; Wlonc, 184 ; a. 315. A.S. *wlanc.*

Wlite, *s.* countenance, appearance, face, beauty, 249 ; hue, 580. A.S. *wlite.*

Wo, *s.* woe, 258.

Woc, *adj.* weak, 581. A.S. *wāc.*

Wod, *adj.* mad, 269, 478. Wode, *def.* the mad man, 648. A.S. *wōd.*

Wode, *s.* wood, 169.

Woke, *adj. pl.* weak, 595. *See* Woc.

Wold, *s.* control ; A wold, at your disposal, 182. A.S. *weald.*

Wolde, *pt. s. subj.* should possess, a. 389. A.S. *wealdan. See* Welden.

Wole, *pr. s.* will, wishes to, 359 ; Wolde, *pt. s.* wished (to do), 283 ; would like (to do), 139, a. 288 ; would desire, 242 ; Wolde, 2 *pt. pl.* would, 27.

Wone, *adj.* wanting, lacking, 57. A.S. *wan.*

Wonin, *v.* dwell, live, 683 ; Woniþ, *pr. s.* resides, 391. A.S. *wunian.*

Word, *s. pl.* words, 418, 419, 491 ; Worde, *dat. s.* speech, 632 ; Wordes, *gen.* of his speech, 301.

Word-wod, *adj.* mad in speech, 281. *See* Wod.

World-ayhte, *s.* worldly wealth, a. 382. *See* Ahte.

Worð, *adj.* worthy, 684. A.S. *weorð.*

Worþe, *in phr.* wel worþe, well be it for, 633. *See* Wurþen.

Worulde, *dat.* the world, 59. A.S. *worold.*

Wot, *pr. s.* knows, 172, 176. A.S. *wāt.*

Wowe, *s.* wrong, adversity, a. 142. A.S. *wōh.*

Woxin, *pp.* grown up, 433 : Woxen, grown, 168. A.S. *weaxen,* pp.

Wrake, *s.* persecution, harm, 142, 647. A.S. *wracu.*

Wraþed, *pp.* angered, 276.

Wreche-dome, *s.* wretchedness, misery, 705.

Wrench, *s.* false notion, lit. deceit, 163 ; Wrenches, *pl.* tricks. A.S. *wrenc.*

Writes, *s. pl.* writings, 67 A.S. *writ.*

Wronge, *adj. pl. as s.* wrongs, 596.

Wroþe, *adj. pl.* evil, perverse, adverse, grievous, a. 115. A.S. *wrãþ.*

Wune þe, *imp. s.* accustom thyself, keep thyself (free), a. 367. A.S. *wunian.*

Wunne, *s.* joy, pleasure, a. 390. A.S. *wyn.*

Wurchen, *ger.* to work, make, procure, 374; to perform, 326; Wurche, 2 *pr. s. subj.* mayst perform, 398. A.S. *wyrcan.*

Wurmes, *pl.* worms, 383. A.S. *wyrm.*

Wurshipe, *s.* worship, honour, 32.

Wurt, *s.* wort, herb, 168. A.S. *wyrt.*

Wurþ, *adj.* worth, a. 314.

Wurþen, *v.* become, be, 184, 299, 436; become, come, 201; Wurþ, *pr. s. as fut.* will (he) be, a. 304; Wurþen, 2 *pr. pl.* become, 487; Wurþien, *v.* come to, go to, 383; Wurþe, *imp. s.* let be, let happen, 571; Wurþu (*for* Wurþ þu), be thou, 269, 478. A.S. *weorþan.*

Wurþin, *v.* worship, 60; Wurþen, *v.* honour, favour, 404. A.S. *weorþian.*

Wurþshipes, *s. pl.* honours, a. 32. A.S. *weorðscipe.*

Wyn-drunken, drunken with wine, 270.

Wyttes, *s. pl.* wits, a. 67. (*But read* writes.)

Ycnoweð, *pr. pl.* know, 672. A.S. *gecnãwan.*

Ydronken, *pp.* drunk, 476. A.S. *gedruncen.*

Yefst, 2 *pr. s.* givest away, a. 182.

Yeorde, *s.* the rod, a. 451. A.S. *gierd, gyrd.*

Yeorne, *adv.* eagerly, a. 101, 107. A.S. *georne.*

Yeue, *v.* give, a. 140.

Yongmon (*read* yong mon), a young man, a. 134.

Youhþe, *dat.* youth, a. 100, 106.

Yuele, *adv.* evilly, ill, 255, 476.

Yuil, *s.* evil, 141. A.S. *yfel.*

Y-werche, *pr. s. subj.* may make, makes, 130. A.S. *gewyrcan.*

Y-wille, *s.* desire, 423. A.S. *gewil, gewile.*

Ywyueth, *pr. s.* wiveth, marries, a. 261. A.S. *gewīfian.*

Ʒe, ye, 27. (MS. *we.*)

Ʒif, if, 292.

Ʒiuen, *v.* give, 140; Ʒef, *imp. s.* 617. A.S. *giefan.*

Ʒu, *acc.* you, 29.

Ʒueþe, *s.* youth, 157.

Ʒung, *adj.* young, 287; Ʒunge, *dat.* to the young, 613.

Ʒure, your, 28.

OXFORD
PRINTED AT THE CLARENDON PRESS
BY HORACE HART, M.A.
PRINTER TO THE UNIVERSITY

ENGLISH

(All books are in extra fcap. 8vo unless otherwise described)

School Dictionaries

Concise Etymological Dictionary, by W. W. Skeat.
A new edition (1901), rewritten throughout and arranged alphabetically. Crown 8vo. 676 pp. 5s. 6d.

Saturday Review:—'Mr. Skeat's larger dictionary has established his title to the gratitude of all scholars; and of his smaller dictionary we can only say that it is not less useful and valuable.'

Student's Dictionary of Anglo-Saxon, by H. Sweet.
Small 4to. 233 pp., printed in 3 columns. 8s. 6d. net.

Notes and Queries:—'For the purpose of the student, no work so trustworthy, so convenient, and so valuable has seen the light.'

Concise Dictionary of Middle English, from A.D. 1150 to A.D. 1580; intended to be used as a glossary to the Clarendon Press Specimens of English Literature, etc.; by A. L. Mayhew and W. W. Skeat. Crown 8vo. 7s. 6d.

Dr. Sweet's Grammars

New English Grammar, logical and historical, in two parts, sold separately: Part I, Introduction, Phonology and Accidence, crown 8vo, second edition, 523 pp., 10s. 6d. Part II, Syntax, crown 8vo, second edition, 146 pp., 3s. 6d.

School World:—'As an English grammar the book is of high value; as an historical study it is of the deepest interest, while its clearness and careful style make it as readable to the literary man as to the grammatical student.'

Short Historical English Grammar. 272 pp. 4s. 6d.

Guardian:—'In the best sense of the word a scholarly book —one that, we hope, will for a long time exercise its influence on the teaching of English.'
Educational Times:—'Excellent in every way.'

Primer of Historical English Grammar, including History of English Phonology, Accidence, Composition, and Derivation, with Specimens of Old, Middle, and Modern English added. 120 pp. 2s.

Dr. Sweet's Primers and Readers

First Steps in Anglo-Saxon, containing 25 pages of grammar, 43 of text, and 40 of explanatory notes. 2s. 6d.

Anglo-Saxon Primer. With grammar and glossary. Eighth edition revised. 126 pp. 2s. 6d.

Anglo-Saxon Reader, in prose and verse. With grammar, metre, notes, and glossary. Seventh edition, revised and enlarged (1898). Crown 8vo. 414 pp. 9s. 6d.

A Second Anglo-Saxon Reader, archaic and dialectal. 220 pp. 4s. 6d.

Old English Reading Primers, being supplements to the Anglo-Saxon Readers.

    I : Selected Homilies of Ælfric. Second edition. 2s.
    II : Extracts from Alfred's Orosius. Second edition. 2s.

First Middle English Primer, with grammar and glossary. Second edition. 2s. 6d.

Second Middle English Primer: extracts from Chaucer, with grammar and glossary. Second edition. 2s. 6d.

Primer of Phonetics. Third edition (1906). 3s. 6d.

    Educational Times :—'A concise, definite and practical primer, eminently the book for a beginner.'

Primer of Spoken English. Second ed. revised. 3s. 6d.

A Book for the Beginner in Anglo-Saxon. By J. EARLE. Fourth edition (1903). 2s. 6d.

A Primer of English Etymology. By W. W. SKEAT. Fourth and revised edition (1904). Stiff covers. 120 pp. 1s. 6d.

A Primer of Classical and English Philology (1905). By W. W. SKEAT. Cloth, 2s.

Annotated Texts
Old and Middle English

Laurence Minot's Poems, edited by J. HALL. Second edition. 4s. 6d.

Gospel of St. Luke in Anglo-Saxon, edited by J. W. BRIGHT. 5s.

Selections from Gower's Confessio Amantis, edited by G. C. MACAULAY (1903). 302 pp. 4s. 6d.

Miracle Plays, Moralities and Interludes, being specimens of the pre-Elizabethan drama, edited, with introduction, notes, and glossary, by A. W. POLLARD. Fourth edition (1903), with ten illustrations. Crown 8vo. 7s. 6d.

Specimens of Early English: with introductions, notes, and glossarial index.

Part I: From *Old English Homilies* to *King Horn* (A.D. 1150 to A.D. 1300): by R. MORRIS. Second edition. 572 pp. 9s.

Part II: From *Robert of Gloucester* to *Gower* (A.D. 1298 to A.D. 1393): by R. MORRIS and W. W. SKEAT. Fourth edition revised. 530 pp. 7s. 6d.

Part III: From the *Ploughman's Crede* to the *Shepheards Calendar* (A.D. 1394 to A.D. 1579): by W. W. SKEAT. Sixth edition. 582 pp. 7s. 6d.

Prof. Skeat's editions

The Oxford Chaucer, containing in one volume the complete text of Chaucer's works; with introduction and glossarial index. Crown 8vo. 906 pp. 3s. 6d. On India paper, from 5s.

The Minor Poems of Chaucer. With notes, etc. Crown 8vo. Second edition. 586 pp. 10s. 6d.

The Hous of Fame. Crown 8vo. 136 pp. 2s.

The Legend of Good Women. Crown 8vo. 286 pp. 6s.

The Prologue, the Knightes Tale, the Nonne Prestes Tale, from the Canterbury Tales. R. MORRIS's edition, re-edited. 324 pp. 2s. 6d.

The Prologue. School edition. 96 pp. 1s.

The Prioresses Tale, Sir Thopas, the Monkes Tale, Clerkes Tale, Squieres Tale, etc. Seventh ed. 412 pp. 4s. 6d.

3

The Tale of the Man of Lawe, the Pardoneres Tale, the Second Nonnes Tale, the Chanouns Yemannes Tale, from the Canterbury Tales. New edition revised (1904). 4s. 6d.

Langland's Piers the Plowman. Sixth edition. 264 pp. 4s. 6d.

The Tale of Gamelyn. Second edition. 104 pp. 1s. 6d.

Wycliffe's Bible : Job, Psalms, Proverbs, Ecclesiastes, and the Song of Solomon. 3s. 6d. The New Testament. 6s.

The Lay of Havelok the Dane (1903). 4s. 6d.

Pierce the Ploughman's Crede (1906). 105 pp. 2s.

The Proverbs of Alfred. In the Press.

The Dream of the Rood, an Old English poem attributed to Cynewulf. Edited by ALBERT S. COOK. 3s. 6d.

Elizabethan

North's Translation of Plutarch's Coriolanus, Cæsar, Brutus, and Antonius, edited, with introduction and notes, by R. H. CARR. Crown 8vo. 3s. 6d. Coriolanus only, 1s. 6d.

More's Utopia, edited, with introduction, notes, and full glossary (by Miss MURRAY), by J. CHURTON COLLINS (1904). Crown 8vo. 3s. 6d.

Elizabethan Critical Essays, selected and edited by GREGORY SMITH : with introduction on the value of Elizabethan criticism and notes. Crown 8vo, 2 vols. 12s. net.

Specimens of the Elizabethan Drama. From Lyly to Shirley, A.D. 1580 to A.D. 1642. Edited, with introductions and notes, by W. H. WILLIAMS. Crown 8vo. 7s. 6d.

The Oxford Shakespeare, containing the complete text of Shakespeare's works, edited, with glossary, by W. J. CRAIG. 3s. 6d. 1264 pp. Crown 8vo. On India paper, from 5s.

Select Plays of Shakespeare. Stiff covers.

Edited by W. G. CLARK and W. ALDIS WRIGHT.

Hamlet. 2s.	Merchant of Venice. 1s.
Macbeth. 1s. 6d.	Richard the Second. 1s. 6d.

Edited by W. ALDIS WRIGHT.

As You Like It. 1s. 6d.	King John. 1s. 6d.
Coriolanus. 2s. 6d.	King Lear. 1s. 6d.
Henry the Eighth. 2s.	Midsummer Night's Dream. 1s. 6d.
Henry the Fifth. 2s.	Much Ado about Nothing. 1s. 6d.
Henry the Fourth, Part I. 2s.	Richard the Third. 2s. 6d.
Julius Caesar. 2s.	Tempest. 1s. 6d.

Twelfth Night. 1s. 6d.

Scenes from Old Play Books, arranged as an Introduction to Shakespeare, by P. SIMPSON. With reproduction of the Swan Theatre. Crown 8vo. 3s. 6d.

Marlowe's Edward II, edited, with introduction and notes, by O. W. TANCOCK. Third edition. 2s. and 3s.

Marlowe's Dr. Faustus and Greene's Friar Bacon and Friar Bungay, edited by A. W. WARD. Fourth edition (1901). Crown 8vo. 448 pp. 6s. 6d.

Spenser's Faery Queene, Books I and II, with introduction and notes by G. W. KITCHIN, and glossary by A. L. MAYHEW. 2s. 6d. each.

Hakluyt's Principal Navigations : being narratives of the Voyages of the Elizabethan Seamen to America. Selection edited by E. J. PAYNE, containing the voyages of Gilbert, Hawkins, Drake, Frobisher, Raleigh and others. Crown 8vo, with portraits. First and second series. Second edition. 324 and 350 pp. 5s. each.

Bacon's Advancement of Learning, edited by W. ALDIS WRIGHT. Crown 8vo, with woodcuts. 424 pp. 3s. 6d.

Shakespeare as a Dramatic Artist. By R. G. MOULTON. Third edition, enlarged. Crown 8vo. 7s. 6d.

Seventeenth Century

The Oxford Milton, edited by H. C. BEECHING. Demy 8vo, with facsimiles, 7s. 6d.; crown 8vo, 3s. 6d.; on India paper, from 5s.; miniature edition, on India paper, 2s. 6d. net.

Milton's Poems, edited by R. C. BROWNE. 422 and 344 pp. Two volumes, 6s. 6d.; or separately, vol. I, 4s., vol. II, 3s.

> **Paradise Lost :** Book I, edited by H. C. BEECHING. 1s. 6d. Book II, edited by E. K. CHAMBERS. 1s. 6d. Together, 2s. 6d.

> **Samson Agonistes,** edited by J. CHURTON COLLINS. Stiff covers. 1s.

In paper covers

Lycidas, 3d.; Comus, 6d.: edited by R. C. BROWNE.   Lycidas, 6d.; L'Allegro, 4d.; Il Penseroso, 4d.; Comus, 1s.: edited by O. ELTON.

> **Areopagitica,** edited by J. W. HALES. 3s.

Bunyan's Pilgrim's Progress, and Grace Abounding, edited, with biographical introduction and notes, by E. VENABLES. Second ed., revised by M. PEACOCK. Cr. 8vo, with portrait. 3s. 6d.

Holy War and the Heavenly Footman, by M. PEACOCK. 3s. 6d.

Clarendon's History of the Rebellion, Book VI, edited by T. ARNOLD. Second edition. Crown 8vo. 5s.

Selections from Dryden, including Astraea Redux, Annus Mirabilis, Absalom and Achitophel, Religio Laici, and The Hind and the Panther: edited by W. D. CHRISTIE. Fifth edition, revised by C. H. FIRTH. 372 pp. 3s. 6d.

Dryden's Essays, selected and edited by W. P. KER (1900). Two volumes crown 8vo. 404 and 324 pp. 10s. 6d.

Dramatic Poesy, edited by T. ARNOLD. Third edition (1904) revised by W. T. ARNOLD. 3s. 6d.

Milton's Prosody, by R. BRIDGES. Crown 8vo. 5s. net.

Eighteenth Century

Locke's Conduct of the Understanding, edited by T. FOWLER. Third edition. 2s. 6d.

Selections from Addison's papers in the Spectator. By T. ARNOLD. 560 pp. 4s. 6d.

Selections from Steele, being papers from the Tatler, Spectator, and Guardian, edited, with introduction, by AUSTIN DOBSON. Second ed. Cr. 8vo, with portrait. 556 pp. 7s. 6d.

Selections from Swift, edited, with biographical introduction and notes, by Sir HENRY CRAIK, containing the greater part of Tale of a Tub, Gulliver's Travels, Battle of the Books, etc. Two volumes crown 8vo, 484 and 488 pp. 7s. 6d. each.

Selections from Pope, with introductions and notes by MARK PATTISON. (1) *Essay on Man,* sixth edition, 1s. 6d. (2) *Satires and Epistles,* fourth edition, 2s.

Parnell's Hermit. Paper covers. 2d.

Thomson's Seasons and the Castle of Indolence, edited by J. Logie Robertson. 4s. 6d. Also *Castle of Indolence* separately. 1s. 6d.

Selections from Gray, edited by Edmund Gosse. 3s. With additional notes for schools by F. Watson. 1s. 6d.

Gray's Elegy and Ode on Eton College. 2d.

Selections from Goldsmith, edited, with introduction and notes, by Austin Dobson. 3s. 6d.

Goldsmith's Traveller, edited by G. Birkbeck Hill. Stiff covers. 1s. *The Deserted Village.* Paper covers. 2d.

Johnson's Rasselas, edited, with introduction and notes, by G. Birkbeck Hill. Cloth flush, 2s.; also 4s. 6d.

> **Rasselas, and Lives of Dryden and Pope,** edited by A. Milnes. 4s. 6d. *Lives* separately. 2s. 6d.

> **Life of Milton,** edited by C. H. Firth. Cloth, 2s. 6d.; stiff covers, 1s. 6d.

> **Vanity of Human Wishes,** ed. by E. J. Payne. 4d.

Selections from Cowper, edited, with a life, introduction, and notes, by H. T. Griffith. 314 and 332 pp.

> Vol. I: Didactic Poems of 1782, with some minor pieces 1779–1783. 3s.

> Vol. II: The Task, with Tirocinium and some minor poems 1784–1799. Third edition. 3s.

Selections from Burke, edited by E. J. Payne.

> I: Thoughts on the Present Discontents: the two Speeches on America. Second edition. 4s. 6d.

> II: Reflections on the French Revolution. Second edition. 5s.

> III: Letters on the proposed Regicide peace. Second ed. 5s.

Selections from Burns, edited, with introduction, notes, and glossary, by J. Logie Robertson. Second edition. 3s. 6d.

Nineteenth Century

Byron's Childe Harold, ed. by H. F. Tozer. 3rd ed. 3s. 6d.

Keats' Odes, edited by A. C. Downer. 3s. 6d. net.

Hyperion, Book I, with notes by W. T. Arnold. 4d.

Scott's Lady of the Lake, edited by W. Minto. 3s. 6d.

Lay of the Last Minstrel, by the same editor. Second edition. 1s. 6d. Canto I. 6d.

Lord of the Isles, edited by T. Bayne. 2s. and 2s. 6d.

Marmion, by the same editor. 3s. 6d.

Old Mortality, edited by H. B. George. Crown 8vo. 2s.

Quentin Durward, edited by P. F. Willert. Crown 8vo. 2s.

Ivanhoe, edited by C. E. Theodosius. Crown 8vo. 2s.

Talisman, edited by H. B. George. Crown 8vo. 2s.

Shelley's Adonais, edited by W. M. Rossetti and A. O. Prickard. Second edition (1904). Crown 8vo. 3s. 6d.

Campbell's Gertrude of Wyoming, edited by H. M. FitzGibbon. Second edition. 1s.

Wordsworth's White Doe of Rylstone, etc., edited by William Knight. 2s. 6d.

Matthew Arnold's Meropé, with *The Electra of Sophocles*, translated by R. Whitelaw: edited by J. Churton Collins. Crown 8vo. 3s. 6d.

Kingsley's Water-Babies, slightly abridged, with illustrations, introduction and notes. Crown 8vo. 3s. 6d.

The Oxford Book of English Verse A.D. 1250–1900. By A. T. Quiller-Couch. 1096 pp. Crown 8vo, gilt top. 7s. 6d. Fcap 8vo, Oxford India paper, cloth extra, gilt top. 10s. 6d.

The Oxford Treasury of English Literature. By G. E. Hadow and W. H. Hadow. Crown 8vo. 3s. 6d. each. Vol. I. Old English to Jacobean. Vol. II. Growth of the Drama.

Typical Selections from the best English writers with introductory notices. Second edition. 3s. 6d. each. Vol. I : Latimer to Berkeley. Vol. II : Pope to Macaulay.

Sentence Analysis. For Lower Forms of Public Schools. By one of the Authors of 'The King's English.' Cr. 8vo. 1s. 6d. net.

Poems of English Country Life, selected and edited by H. B. George and W. H. Hadow. Crown 8vo. 2s.

OXFORD: AT THE CLARENDON PRESS